must sees
Prague

Old Town Square/©Prague Information Service

mustsees **Prague**

Editorial Manager	Jonathan P. Gilbert
Editor	M. Linda Lee
Writer	Fiona Gaze
Production Manager	Natasha G. George
Cartography	John Dear
Photo Editor	Yoshimi Kanazawa
Photo Research	Sean Sachon
Layout	Chris Bell, cbdesign, Natasha G. George
Interior Design	Chris Bell, cbdesign
Cover Design	Chris Bell, cbdesign, Natasha G. George

Contact Us

Michelin Travel and Lifestyle
One Parkway South
Greenville, SC 29615
USA
www.michelintravel.com
michelin.guides@usmichelin.com

Michelin TravelPartner
Hannay House
39 Clarendon Road
Watford, Herts WD17 1JA
UK
(01923) 205 240
www.ViaMichelin.com
travelpubsales@uk.michelin.com

Special Sales

For information regarding bulk sales, customized
editions and premium sales, please contact
our Customer Service Departments:

USA	1-800-432-6277
UK	(01923) 205 240
Canada	1-800-361-8236

Michelin Apa Publications Ltd

58 Borough High Street, London SE1 1XF, United Kingdom

No part of this publication may be reproduced in any form
without the prior permission of the publisher.

© 2012 Michelin Apa Publications Ltd
ISBN 978-1-907099-75-5
Printed: December 2011
Printed and bound: Himmer, Germany

Note to the reader:

Café Obecní dům, Municipal House

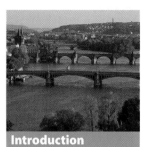

Introduction

TABLE OF CONTENTS

★★★ ATTRACTIONS

Unmissable historic, cultural and natural sights

Old Jewish Cemetery p 78

©Rod Purcell/Apa Publications

National Theater p 116

©Rod Purcell/Apa Publications

Church of St. Nicholas p 66

©Prague Information Service

Lesser Town p 45

©Robert Harding Produc/age fotostock

Old Town p 36

©Prague Information Service

Charles Bridge p 62

©Prague Information Service

Strahov Library p 71

©Chad Ehlers/age fotostock

STAR ATTRACTIONS

Le Palais p 151

©Hotel Le Palais Prague

Bohemian crystal p 121

©Rod Purcell/Apa Publications

Czech wines p 123, 126

©Vinograf

Bike the city p 114

©Rod Purcell/Apa Publications

Horse-drawn carriage rides   p 110

©Private Prague Guide

Visit a mall   p 123

©Rod Purcell/Apa Publications

Červená tabulka   p 138

©Karel Vladyka/Červená tabulka

Climb Petřín Tower   p 111

©Prague Information Service

STAR ATTRACTIONS

★★★ ATTRACTIONS

Unmissable historic, cultural and natural sights

For more than 75 years p eop le have used Michelin stars to take the guesswork out of travel. Our star-rating system help s you make the best decision on where to go, what to do, and what to see.

★★★	Unmissable
★★	Worth a trip
★	Worth a detour
No star	Recommended

ACTIVITIES

Unmissable activities, entertainment, restaurants and hotels
We recommend all of the activities in this guide, but our top picks are highlighted with the Michelin Man logo.

STAR ATTRACTIONS

IDEAS AND TOURS

Throughout this guide, you will find inspiration for a thousand different holidays in Prague. The following is a selection of ideas to start you on your way. Many sites in bold can be found in the Index.

Walking Tours

The best way to experience Prague is by foot, and a guided tour lets you take in the sights and information at the same time. There are countless companies that offer tours, but these are some of the best ones.

Prague Free Tour

Yes, a free tour – and an ideal way to see the city for anyone on a budget. Led by a young, relaxed group of friendly and knowledgeable guides, these tours have meeting points around the city in Old Town, New Town and Lesser Town (you can join in wherever you want). Tours are offered daily, with pick-up at 10:30am and 1:45pm outside the Starbucks on Old Town Square (look for the guides wearing red T-shirts). The company also offers a tour of Prague Castle for 300 Kč *(www.newpraguetours.com).*

Prague Tours, Walks and Excursions

This company is the oldest private walking-tour provider in Prague. You'll spot their groups, led by a guide holding an umbrella, throughout the Old Town, New Town, Lesser Town and beyond. Of several routes they cover, the **Ultimate Tour** leads you on foot, by tram and by boat through the city for a thorough six-hour exploration of Prague, and includes refreshments and a three-course lunch at a traditional Czech restaurant. The daily tour departs at 10:30am from Wenceslas Square 56 *(1,200 Kč; 775 369 121; www.praguer.com).*

Jewish Quarter

One of Europe's most significant heritage sights, Prague's **Jewish Town★★★** has a fascinating and moving history. On the **Prague Experience** company's tour of

Prague by boat

©Prague Information Service

this quarter, you'll discover the traditions, customs and legends of the Jewish people in Prague and learn about the everyday life of the former ghetto's inhabitants – their poverty, successes and isolation. The 2.5-hour tour, which costs 550 Kč, includes access and admission to all of the sites under the auspices of the Jewish Museum. The meeting place in Old Town is confirmed once you book your tour *(tours run Sun–Fri at 11am; www.pragueexperience.com).*

Architecture Tour

Guide-prague.cz offers a tour of Prague's architectural sights called **Ten Centuries of the Architecture of Prague**. The three-hour tour points out examples of Romanesque, Gothic, Renaissance, Baroque, Classical and Art Nouveau architectural styles, as well as Cubism, Functionalism and contemporary architecture *(2,790 Kč for 1–4 persons; discounts available for larger groups; 776 868 770; guide-prague.cz).*

Other Organized Tours
Bus Tours

There's a lot of ground to cover in Prague, literally and figuratively. For a relaxed way to make sure you see all the sights, **Martin Tour Prague** is a good bet. In addition to a selection of guided walking tours, the company offers private rental of an eight-seat open-top minibus, with a driver to navigate through the maze of medieval streets, so you don't have to. Tours can be customized according to what you would most like to see *(1,500 Kč/hr; 224 212 473; www.martintour.cz).*

Architecture Tour, Dancing House

©Patricia Grube/Michelin

Ghost Tours

Prague is a tangibly spine-tingling place, with more than its fair share of myths, legends and creepy historical happenings. The sepia glow of lantern lights on the cobblestone streets is the perfect setting for a ghost tour of the city, a great way to see the darker side of Prague. **McGee's Ghost Tours** offers several haunting excursions, including Ghost Tours & Legends, Haunted History of the Bridge, Prague Castle After Dark, and Haunted Pubs Walk. The one-hour **Ghost Tours & Legends** goes daily, year-round, and features a narrative tale of Prague's spooky history *(departs at 7pm, 9 pm & 10:15pm Jun–Sept; 300 Kč; 723 306 963; www.mcgeesghosttours.com).*

Prague by Segway

Led in small groups by friendly guides, **Prague Segway Tours** save your soles by allowing you to zip around Prague's main attractions via Segway, and cover more ground in a shorter time than you would on a walking tour. **Group tours** come with an English-speaking guide and take approximately 2.5 to 3 hours; **City Segway Tours** depart at 9am and 2pm, while the Sunset Segway Tour leaves at 7pm *(1,490 Kč for either tour)*. For 1,925 Kč, you can book a spot on the **Alchemal Prague Tour**, which uncovers the city's magical past. Private tours are also available *(724 280 838; www.prague-segway-tours.com)*.

Theme Tours

There's no shortage of things to see in Prague, but sometimes it helps to be pointed in the right direction. Below are a few suggestions for theme-based self-guided tours. If you prefer to fashion your own itinerary, the website for the **Prague Information Service** *(www.praguewelcome.cz)* has an interactive function where you can input how long you will be in the city, and it will tailor an itinerary to your schedule, complete with a printable map.

Lesser Town Bridge Towers

©Prague Information Service

The Royal Route

This path, delineated by a bronze line on the pavement, marks the coronation route that most Czech kings traveled between 1438 and 1863. Originally, it connected the Royal Court with Prague Castle. Today, it is one of the best routes to follow for a self-guided walking tour of Prague's main sights. It starts in **Old Town★★★** at the **Powder Tower★**, where the Royal Court used to sit at the site now occupied by the **Municipal House★★★**. The route then goes through **Old Town Square★★★**, past the **Astronomical Clock★★★** and the **Old Town Hall★** and then down **Karlova★★** (Charles Street). From there, it crosses the **Charles Bridge★★★** into the **Lesser Town★★★** and goes across **Mostecká** (Bridge Street). It continues along **Nerudova★★** (Neruda Street) through **Lesser Town Square★** and ends up at **Prague Castle★★★**. Walking this circuit is a wonderful way to admire the city's incredible architecture and to get a feel for its history.

Prague Pub Crawl

The Golden City is a mecca not only for beer lovers, but for anyone looking to party. If you're at least 18 years old, the Prague Pub Crawl offers an organized visit to four pubs and one nightclub in a safe and amiable group environment. Meet at the Prague Pub Crawl's pub at Dlouha 24 near Old Town Square, and visit a series of pubs in Old Town before winding up at **Karlovy lázně** *(see Nightlife)*, one of Europe's biggest nightclubs. The price of 490 Kč includes drinks along the way – Czech beer,

View from St. Vitus Cathedral

©Prague Information Service

Bohemian absinthe, Moravian wine and vodka shooters – as well as VIP access to the music lounge. They'll even order pizza for you in case you get the munchies *(tours depart nightly between 10pm–10:30pm; 731 067 775; www.pubcrawl.cz)*.

Best Views of the City

For some of the most stunning views over the Prague skyline, walk the path that runs between **Petřín Park** *(see Parks and Gardens)* and Prague Castle, in either direction. If you're starting at Petřín, take the funicular up to the top, where you can climb **Petřín Tower** for a bird's-eye view over the city. Then follow the path that wanders through the park and passes **Vojan Park**, past the entrance to **Strahov Monastery** and over to **Castle Square★★**.

There's another stellar view of Prague from the top of the lofty **Žižkov TV Tower** *(Mahlerovy sady 1, Žižkov; Metro A: Jiřího z Poděbrad; observation deck open daily 10am–10pm; 120 Kč; 724 251 286; www.praguerocket.cz.)*.

Quick Trips

Stuck for ideas? Try these:

IDEAS AND TOURS

15

CALENDAR OF EVENTS

At practically any time of the year, there is some sort of event or festival going on in or around Prague. During these events, the streets come to life, and the arts become a tangible thing that breathes new life into the city. Listed below is a selection of Prague's most popular annual events and festivals. Dates and times vary, so be sure to check in advance with the **Prague Tourism Board:** *www.praguewelcome.cz/en* or *221 714 444.*

January

New Year's Day
January 1
On this public holiday, fireworks displays explode into the sky at 6pm from Letna, an elevated area near Prague Castle. For the best views, head toward the river *(www.pragueexperience.com).*

Prague Winter Music Festival
early January
For decades, this festival has brought opera and ballet classics alive in the dark days of winter, usually in the first week of January *(various venues; www.praguewinter.com).*

Days of European Film
late January – early February
Beginning in late January, this festival highlights some 30 different European films at many cinemas in the city center, both multiplexes and art houses. You may even see some of the stars, directors and producers *(various venues; www.eurofilmfest.cz/en).*

February

Masopust
week before Ash Wednesday
The local incarnation of Mardi Gras (Masopust is Czech for "meat-fast") brings everyone out on the streets for a party. The Prague version includes parades featuring elaborate handmade costumes, as well as pig-roasts, theater performances and family activities. Events take place in various districts of Prague *(www.carnevale.cz).*

Matějská pouť
late February–April
Starting either in late February or early March and running through

June: Prague Proms

©Martin Malý

the end of April, "Crazy Day" at the Výstaviště fairgrounds comes alive with lights and colors as carnival rides and games arrive for a truly entertaining and family-friendly run *(Holešovice; www.matejskapout.cz)*.

March/April

Easter Markets
March 24–April 15
Several weeks before Easter, Old Town Square and Wenceslas Square spring to colorful life with stalls strewn with handmade Easter eggs, wooden toys and traditional snacks *(www. pragueexperience.com)*.

Witches' Night
(Paleni Carodejnic)
April 30
At this ancient folk festival, bonfires are lit and effigies burned in a playful ritual celebrating the end of winter. Costumed events go on at many Prague parks, but the most famous one is on Petřín Hill *(www.pragueexperience.com)*.

May

Prague Marathon
May 13
Some 20,000 runners show up for this international marathon, which starts and finishes in Old Town Square. In addition to the main event, the weekend's festivities include a mini-marathon *(4.2km/2.6mi)* for families and an eco walk *(www.praguemarathon.com)*.

Prague Spring International Music Festival
May–early June
For three weeks, this wildly popular classical concert series holds sway at various venues around the city. Be sure to reserve tickets in advance *(www.festival.cz)*.

Czech Beer Festival
mid-May–early June
Breweries come from all over the Czech Republic to present their liquid wares at this Oktoberfest-inspired event. Expect beer-hall seating in big tents, live music and lots of Czech food *(PVA Letňany Exhibition Center; www.pivnifestivalpraha.cz)*.

Mezi ploty
last weekend in May
"Between the Fences" is a music and theater festival held on the grounds of a psychiatric hospital. Many famous Czech acts and theater troupes turn out to heighten awareness of mental illness *(Psychiatrická léčebna in Bohnice; www.meziploty.cz)*.

Prague Food Festival
last weekend in May
This three-day festival, run by the respected authors of a local restaurant guide, touts Prague's different cuisines through the offerings of more than 30 of the country's best restaurants *(Royal Garden of Prague Castle; www.grand-restaurant.cz)*.

June

Prague Fringe Festival
early June
This ten-day festival of theater and comedy, based on the famous Edinburgh Fringe Festival, brings innovative and experimental performances to intimate, unusual venues around Prague, with an interesting lineup of amateurs and professionals that changes every year *(various venues; www.praguefringe.com)*.

17

United Islands of Prague
late June

In June, a festival highlighting various musical genres takes place on the many islands on Prague's Vltava River for several days of merriment (*various venues; www.unitedislands.cz*).

Tanec Praha
last week in June

This modern-dance festival highlights the best of local and visiting international talent, including up-and-coming stars of the local dance scene (*various venues; www.tanecpha.cz*).

Karlovy Vary International Film Festival
late June – first week in July

Cinephiles from the world over flock to the west Bohemian spa town of Karlovy Vary for this Cannes-like film festival, one of Europe's most accessible to people not in the industry (*various venues; www.kviff.com*).

Prague Proms
late June–late July

Inspired by the London BBC Proms, Prague Proms brings together symphony in all its forms. A highlight is the **Hollywood Nights** event, which shows off music's role in the making of a film. The festival is affiliated with the Czech National Symphony Orchestra (*various venues; www.pragueproms.cz*).

July

Bohemia Jazz Fest
mid-July

Stars of the European jazz scene converge on Prague in July, jazzing up venues like Old Town Square for nightly concerts (*various venues; www.bohemiajazzfestival.cz*).

A Summer Nights Dream
late July

At this festival, called Sen Letní Noci in Czech, Balkan brass bands and some of the biggest names in Czech music perform on a floating barge on the river. Spectators line the embankments to listen and dance, and those with boats cram the river for a closer look (*Vltava River, between the Charles and Legionnaire's bridges; www.senletninoci.cz*).

Summer Festivities of Early Music
late July–early August

This series of unique concerts focuses on the styles of music throughout history in the Czech lands; it pairs music with historic venues (*various venues; www.letnislavnosti.cz/en*).

August/September

Verdi Festival
August

Celebrating the 19C Italian composer Guiseppe Verdi, this month-long festival opens the opera season each year with a run of Verdi's most beloved operas (*Prague State Opera, Legerova 75; www.opera.cz*).

July: Bohemia Jazz Fest

©bohemiajazzfestival.cz

Teatotroc Street Theater Festival

early September

Theater takes to the streets in this festival of pantomime, juggling, stilt-walking and marionette shows on Kampa Island. Theater companies from around the world give some 80 performances over a few days *(Kampa Island; www.teatrotoc.eu)*.

Vinobrani

early September

Throughout September, wine-making towns around the country celebrate the grape harvest. Wine shops stay open late pouring the *burčák*, the new wine, accompanied by song and dance. The wine region of South Moravia is the best place to enjoy Vinobrani, and the wine capitals of **Znojmo** and **Mikulov** hold their events on different weekends. **Mělník** is the closest wine town to Prague for a day trip *(www.vinobrani.cz)*.

Dvořák's Prague Festival

early–late September

Over the course of several weeks, the Rudolfinum hosts a series of concerts in honor of Czech composer Antonín Dvořák. Works by the likes of Mozart, Schubert and Strauss are also included *(Alšovo nábřeží 79/12; www.dvorakovapraha.cz)*.

Prague Autumn International Music Festival

mid-September–mid-October

One of Europe's top billings, Prague Autumn welcomes conductors from all over the world to play with the Czech Philharmonic and the Prague Symphony Orchestra. *(Rudolfinum, Alšovo nábřeží 79/12; www.strunypodzimu.cz)*.

October

Prague International Jazz Festival

mid-October–mid-November

The first festival by this name took place in 1964, and since then the event has developed a life of its own. Today it features everything from jazz greats to Big Bands *(various venues; www.jazzfestivalpraha.cz)*.

November/December

Czech Press Photo

November–January

A prestigious collection of award-winning photographs is displayed at this free exhibition. Works illustrate the past year's most moving documentation of global and local events as well as great artistic achievement in the photographic media *(Old Town Hall; www.czechpressphoto.cz)*.

Christmas Markets

month of December

Markets open on the last weekend in November, with the main markets being in Old Town Square and Wenceslas Square. The biggest event takes place on December 1, when the Christmas tree on Old Town Square is lit, accompanied by music *(various venues in Prague; www.pragueexperience.com)*.

New Year's Eve

December 31

If rowdy and loud is how you like your New Year's Eve, then come hear the concerts on Wenceslas Square, watch the free fireworks burst over the river, and join the masses partying in the streets of downtown Prague *(www.pragueexperience.com)*.

CALENDAR OF EVENTS

PRACTICAL INFORMATION

WHEN TO GO

Prague is a city for all seasons, and each has its own distinct charm. With a temperate climate typical of this central region of Bohemia, Prague sees pleasantly warm summers, when temperatures can range between 20°C and 30°C (68°F–86°F) and thunderstorms are a regular occurrence (May through August are the rainiest months). Temperatures tend to cool off in early August, usually brightening up into an Indian summer in September. Autumn and spring offer milder weather with little rain, and there are numerous outdoor festivals throughout these seasons. Because it is a landlocked country, the Czech Republic is not a destination for beach lovers; however, there are plenty of lakes around the country that are great for swimming in summer.

In winter, temperatures can dip below 4°C (24°F), but the holiday season in Prague is always magical. Snow-covered rooftops add to the romantic air of the city, and Charles Bridge takes on a unique beauty during a snow flurry. Another holiday treat, the **Christmas Markets** run through December *(see Calendar of Events)*.

KNOW BEFORE YOU GO
Useful Websites

www.czechtourism.com – The Czech tourism board's official website, with comprehensive information in English.

www.praguewelcome.cz – The Prague tourism board's official website offers information about accommodations and restaurants.

www.prague.net/prague-disabled-mobility – A comprehensive list of metro stops and trams that cater to disabled visitors.

www.dpp.cz/en – The English website for the Prague Integrated Transport (PIT) system lists maps, schedules and fares for trams, buses and the subway.

Tourism Offices

Prague Information Service (PIS), the city's main tourist information bureau, provides maps and information about attractions, tours, accommodations and more. There are **two main offices** in Old Town: **Old Town Hall** on Old Town Square *(open daily 9am–7pm; 221 714 444; www.prague-info.cz/en)*, and at **Rytírská 31** *(open Mon–Sat*

Traveling with Pets

If you are traveling with a pet, you will need identification of the animal (a microchip or similar marking), a passport for special-interest breeding animals, and certification of vaccination against rabies.

Average Seasonal Temperatures in Prague				
	Jan	**Apr**	**Jul**	**Oct**
Avg. High	34°F/1°C	54°F/12°C	72°F/22°C	54°F/12°C
Avg. Low	24°F/-4°C	36°F/2°C	54°F/12°C	39°F/4°C

10am–6pm, Sun noon–4pm).
There are other locations at the Lesser Town Bridge Tower and at the Main Train Station *(Wilsonova 8, New Town)*, as well as at the international airport.

International Visitors
Czech Embassies Abroad
Washington – 3900 Spring of Freedom St., NW, Washington, DC 20008, USA. (202) 274-9100. www.mzv.cz/washington.
London – 26–30 Kensington Palace Gardens, London, UK W8 4QY. (+44) 20 7243 1115. www.mzv.cz/london.
Sydney – 169 Military Road, Dover Heights, Sydney, NSW 2030. (+61) 2 9581 0111. www.mzv.cz/Sydney.

Foreign Embassies in Prague
American Embassy – Tržiště 15, Lesser Town. (+420) 257 022 000. prague.usembassy.gov.
Australian Consulate – 6th Floor, Solitaire Building, Klimentska ul 10, New Town. (+420) 221 729 260. www.dfat.gov.au/missions/countries/cz.html.
British Embassy – Thunovska 14, Lesser Town. (+420) 257 402 370. www.ukinczechrepublic.fco.gov.uk/en.

Entry Requirements
Passports and Visas
The Czech Republic became a member of the European Union in 2004. In 2007, it joined the Shengen zone of border-free travel countries. Citizens of EU countries, Iceland, Norway, Liechtenstein and Switzerland can travel within the Czech Republic without a visa. A travel document or valid EU ID card is sufficient to enter. If you plan to stay longer than three months you must notify the foreign police service. Citizens of countries that have a visa-waiver agreement with the Czech Republic, of which the United States and Canada are included, need only bring a passport valid for at least six months from the date of entry. All other citizens must apply for a visa at their local Czech embassy.

Customs Regulations
Since joining the European Union, customs checks at the Czech borders have ended. You will, however, encounter customs officers when arriving on an international flight. Goods – valued up to €300 ($412) and excluding tobacco and alcohol products – brought into the European Union for personal use are exempt from customs duty. When arriving by air, the limit is €430 ($590) per person. If you are bringing cash into the Czech Republic in excess of €10,000 ($13,730), you will need to notify the customs authority of this in writing.

Visitors can freely bring in the following: 200 cigarettes or 100 cigars of up to 3 grams, 50 cigars, or 250 grams of smoking tobacco; 1 liter of alcohol or spirits over 22% alcohol by volume, 2 liters of fortified or sparkling wine, or 2 liters of still wine; 50 grams of perfume.

Restricted items include meat, meat products, milk and dairy products and certain plants and wildlife. Narcotics, weapons, explosives and pornographic materials are **strictly prohibited**.

VAT Refunds

All goods and services in the Czech Republic are subject to a value-added tax (VAT), which is reflected in the advertised price of goods. The standard rate of 19% is charged on all goods and services; a reduced rate of 9% is charged for certain items such as food products, pharmaceuticals, printed books and periodicals. The VAT on products purchased for private, noncommercial use can be reclaimed, unless you are a citizen or a permanent resident of a European Union country and you are returning to a European Union country.

For more information about the VAT refund, check online at the website of the **Customs Administration of the Czech Republic**: www.celnisprava.cz.

Health

There are multiple state and private health centers in Prague. A European health-insurance card will be needed for any European Union (EU) citizens that visit a hospital (charges apply). If you are not a permanent resident of the EU, you will need to provide the health facility with your private insurance details. If you do not have this, you will have to pay for any treatment in cash. There are no recommended vaccinations that you need to have before traveling to Prague.

Tourist Health Services

Doctor Prague Health Centre – Vodickova 28, 2nd floor, New Town. Open daily 24 hours. 224 220 040 or 603 433 833/603 (24hr hotline).
Emergency Dental Service – Palackeho 5, New Town. Open Mon & Wed 8am–5:30pm, Tue & Thu 8am–4pm, Fri 8am–2pm. 224 235 085.
Or contact **American Dental Associates** (*V Celnici 4; 221 18 11 21; www.americandental.cz*).

Pharmacies

Pharmacies are plentiful on any of the main streets around Prague. Look for buildings with a green neon cross out front, and the word *lékárna* ("pharmacy" in Czech). Registered pharmacists generally work from 9am–6pm Monday through Friday.

GETTING THERE
By Air

The primary international airport for Czech Republic is **Prague-Ruzyně** (*PRG; 17km/10.5mi north of the city; 220 113 314; www.prg. aero/en*), located about a 30-minute drive from the city center. There are three terminals at the airport; Terminals 1 and 2 are used for international and domestic departures and arrivals, while Terminal 3 is reserved for general and business aviation. When you exit immigration and customs, you will see hotel information desks. There are plenty of ATMs in the airport, and we recommend that you withdraw Czech crowns here rather than changing your money at a bank or an exchange bureau.

Airlines

A number of airlines serve Prague-Ruzyně from major cities around Europe and America.

Aer Lingus
Mala Stupartska 7, New Town
+420 224 815 373
www.aerlingus.com

Czech Airlines
V Celnici 5, New Town
+420 239 007 007
www.czechairlines.com

Delta
Národní 58/32, New Town
+420 224 946 731
www.delta.com

Emirates
Na Příkopě 859/22, New Town
+420 239 016 320
www.emirates.com

Airport Transfers

Taxi – Metered taxis wait outside the terminals. A taxi from the airport to the city center takes about 30 minutes and costs 500 Kč to 600 Kč. If you are going farther east or south, this price may rise to 900 Kč. Beware that some Czech taxi drivers tamper with the meters to make them run up faster when driving tourists. **AAA Taxi** and **City Taxi** are both reputable companies that operate at the airport.

Bus – Prague public transport offers a cheaper way to get to the center, though this mode of transportation requires a few changes along the way.

Bus no. 119 will drop you outside the metro station Dejvická *(a 25–30min trip)*. This bus leaves every 10–20 minutes from both terminals 1 and 2 *(a 25–30min trip)*. From here, you can access the Metro A line, which passes through the city center.

Bus no. 100 leaves every 15–30 minutes for Zlicin *(a 20min trip)*, from which point you can take the Metro B line to the center.

Bus no. 179 departs from the airport every 15–30 minutes for the Metro B stop at Nové Butovice *(a 45min trip)*.

> **Budget Flights**
> **Easyjet** is the main budget airline operating out of Prague Airport, especially for flights to and from the United Kingdom *(www.easyjet.com)*.

Bus no. 510 is the night bus that services the airport. If your flight arrives between midnight and 3:30am, you will need to take this bus, which goes to the Metro B Stodůlky station.

Metro – There are no subways or trains currently servicing Prague-Ruzyně airport, although there are plans to build a link in the future.

By Bus

The two main **bus stations** in Prague are **Florenc** *(Křižíkova 4–6, Florenc; www.florenc.cz)* and **Na Knížecí** *(Smichov)*.
If you are taking an international bus, you will most likely be using the Florenc station, which is located on the Metro C and B lines. Bus times and ticket prices can be found online at: **www.idos.cz**. Many bus companies offer competitive fares both domestically and internationally; the best is the **Student Agency** *(www.studentagency.cz)*, which has a modern fleet of buses that feature movies, refreshments and free Wi-Fi.

GETTING AROUND
By Public Transportation

The **Prague Public Transport Company** *(www.dpp.cz/en)* runs an extensive network of subways, buses and trams.

DAYTIME SERVICE

METRO A

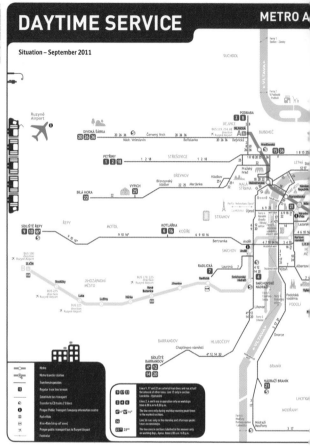

Situation – September 2011

Metro

There are three Metro lines in Prague: the **A (Green) line** runs from southeast to northwest; the **B (Yellow) line** runs from northeast to southwest; and the **C (Red) line** runs from north to south. Lines intersect at one of three transfer stations: Můstek, Florenc and Muzeum. Transfers are clearly marked and take about 5 minutes walking time. Trains run from 5am to midnight on weekdays and until 1am on weekends. There are two types of short-term **tickets**: a 30-minute ticket *(24 Kč)* and a 90-minute ticket *(32 Kč)*. These tickets are valid for one trip but can be used on any type of public transport within the city, and they include transfers. If you're going to be in the city for a few days, you can buy a 24-hour pass *(110 Kč)* or a three-day pass *(310*

infolinka
296 19 18 17
www.dpp.cz

Dopravní podnik
hlavního města Prahy

PRAŽSKÁ
INTEGROVANÁ
DOPRAVA

PRACTICAL INFORMATION

Kč). Tickets for the Metro can be purchased from the machines by the entrance escalators; note that tickets must be validated after purchase with a stamp from the little yellow machines nearby.

Bus

City buses primarily service the outskirts of Prague, with the metro and trams covering the center. Buses in the city run from 4:30am–midnight, with buses leaving at 6- to 8-minute intervals at peak times and 10- to 20-minute intervals at nonpeak times. On weekends, the interval is more like 20–30 minutes. Night buses are also available from midnight until 4:30am. Check online at www.idos.cz for schedules and ticket prices.

Tram

You can get to almost all parts of the city on Prague's comprehensive tram system. Daytime trams run from 4:30am–midnight in 8- to 10-minute intervals (8–15 minutes on weekends). Night trams (numbers 51 to 58) run from midnight–4:30am at 40-minute intervals. Ticket prices are the same for trams as they are for the Metro. Not all tram stops have ticket machines; you can purchase tickets in shops and tobacconists around the city center and also at all Metro stops.

By Train

There are a number of train stations in Prague that have international departures and arrivals. These include the **Main Station** (Hlavní nádraží; *Wilsonova 8, New Town*) located on the Metro C line, **Holešovice Station** (Nádraží Holešovice; *Vrbenského ul., Holešovice*) also on the Metro C line, and **Smíchov Station** (Smíchovské Nádraží; *Nádražní ul., at Rozkošného, Smíchov*) located on the Metro B line. Trains can get you to most other countries in Central Europe and beyond; plus they're a cheap way of getting to different parts of the Czech Republic. It is possible to get around Prague using trains, though it is not the most convenient method. For ticket and time schedule information, check online at *www.idos.cz*.

By Car

If you are planning to drive a car in the Czech Republic, you will need a European or International driver's license, an ID card (European Union citizens) or a valid passport and proper documentation. Required vehicle documents include a certificate of road-worthiness, a third-party insurance card and a green card. For driving on Czech highways, you must purchase a special permit sticker, available at most gas stations.

Rental Cars

Many of the big international rental-car agencies have offices at Prague Airport and in the city center. You must be at least 18 years of age and present a valid passport or picture ID and a valid driver's license from your country of origin in order to rent a car.

Rules of the Road

* Vehicles are driven on the right side of the road in the Czech Republic.
* Seat belts must be worn by all passengers while driving.
* Headlights must be on at all times, no matter the conditions.
* Drinking and driving is strictly prohibited. In the Czech Republic, it is illegal to drive after drinking any amount of alcohol.
* It is against the law to use your mobile phone while driving.

Prague tram

©Prague Public Transport Company, Inc.

MUST KNOW

Car Rental		
Car Rental Company	✆ **Reservations**	**Internet**
Avis	235 362 420	www.avis.com
Budget	220 113 253	ww.budget.com
CS Czechocar	220 113 454	www.czechocar.cz
Dvorak	220 113 676	www.dvorak-rentacar.cz
Europcar	220 113 207	www.europcar.com
Hertz	225 345 021	www.hertz.com
Sixt	220 115 346	www.sixt.com

+ Pedestrians have the right of way at crosswalks; sometimes people will walk straight out in front of vehicles, so pay special attention.

Accidents

If you are involved in an accident in the Czech Republic, you do not need to call the police if you think that costs for damage to the vehicles amount to less than 100,000 Kč ($5,500), and if the participants agree on who caused the accident. You do need to fill out the standard European Accident Statement form (your insurance company can provide you with this) to record the accident and submit it to the local police station.

By Taxi

Prague taxi drivers have a bad reputation for trying to take advantage of unsuspecting tourists. Although the situation is getting better, your best bet is to use the more reputable companies. It is best to call for a taxi by phone, rather than hailing one on the street. Here are the names and numbers of the most trusted taxi companies in Prague:

AAA Radiotaxi – 140 14 or 222 333 222; www.aaa-taxi.cz.
City Taxi – 257 257 257; www.citytaxi.cz.
Halotaxi – 244 114 411; www.halotaxi.cz.
Profi Taxi – 140 35 or 2 61 31 41 51; www.profitaxi.cz.
Sedop – 777 666 333; www.sedop.cz.

By Bicycle

Prague streets are probably not the safest place to bike for people not familiar with the city; however, there are several well-maintained bike paths. You can rent bikes for the day in numerous parks around the city *(see The Great Outdoors)*.

ACCESSIBILITY

Prague is not the easiest city to navigate for people with disabilities. Cobblestone streets present challenges to wheelchairs, and few public toilets accommodate wheelchairs. In addition, many older buildings do not have elevators. As for public transit, about half the Metro stations have accessible elevators, and new trams and buses are equipped with street-level entry doors.

For information on wheelchair access and special-needs transportation, **visit www.dpp.cz/en** or **www.prague.net/prague-disabled-mobility**.

You can also inquire at the **Prague Association of Wheelchair Users** *(Benediktská 6; 224 827 210; www.pov.cz)*.

BASIC INFORMATION
Accommodations

For a list of suggested lodgings, see Must Stay. The **Prague Information Service** *(www.prague-info.cz/en)* maintains an online hotel directory; for reservations, the site links to booking.com for some hotels.

Hostels

No-frills hostels are a great choice for budget travelers. A bed in a dorm-style room starts as low as 246 Kč/$13 in Prague, which has more than a dozen hostels and low-cost lodgings. For details, see **www.prague-hostels.cz**.

Touring Tip

Many hotels and hostels offer special package and seasonal deals throughout the year. Check the list of websites in *Must Stay* to make sure that you are getting the best deal possible.

Business Hours
Banks

Banks are open Monday to Friday from 8am or 9am to 4pm or 5pm.

Attractions

Most attractions and museums are open Tuesday through Sunday from 10am–6pm. Exceptions include the Jewish museums and synagogues, which are closed on Saturday.

Discounts

Many museums and other attractions in Prague offer discounts to students and seniors. Museums also offer a reduced family rate for two adults and one or more children.

Shops

Most shops stay open from 9am until 6pm. Larger supermarkets and family-run corner shops tend to stay open later (9pm or 10pm), and there are several that are open 24 hours, especially in the city center. Malls and shopping centers are generally open until 10pm. Some shops close for lunch at noon or 1pm, but most stay open all day.

Pharmacies

Pharmacies, or *lékárna* in Czech, usually open at 8am. Some stay open until 6pm, while others stay

---

Prague Card

If your plans include visits to many museums, consider purchasing a Prague Card *(790 Kč/adult, 550 Kč/child; www.praguecitycard.com)*.

Valid for four days, the card allows free admission to more than 40 of the city's top attractions (with the exception of sites within the Jewish Museum complex) in addition to savings in designated shops and on city tours.

Buy a Prague Card at the **Prague Information Service** (PIS) center at the Old Town Hall *(Staroměstské náměstí 1/3)* and other locations, as well as at the airport and certain hotels in the city.

open as late as 8pm. Pharmacies that are open 24 hours a day:

Lékárna Palackého – Palackého 5, New Town; 224 946 982.

Lékárna U Svaté Ludmily – Belgická 37, Vinohrady; 222 513 396.

Lékárna Letná – Františka Křížka 22, Letná; 233 375 573.

Lékárna Berytos – Vítězné nám 13, Dejvice; 224 325 520.

Electricity

The electricity network in the Czech Republic has a voltage of 230 V and frequency of 50 Hz. Plug sockets have two round holes and one round pin. If you have a universal recharger, all you'll need is a simple connector with your system on one end and the Czech system on the other end. If your appliance works on another voltage, you will need an adapter. These can be purchased at shops or in the airport, or borrowed from your hotel.

Internet

In the city center, many of Prague's pubs, cafés and restaurants offer free Wi-Fi Internet access; just ask your server for the network password. There are a number of Internet cafés around Prague,

though they are not as numerous as in other cities.

Laws and Safety

Prague is a modern and safe European city, but when traveling to any big city, it is advisable to be cautious. Although pickpockets can be a problem in Prague, violent crime is not a common occurrence, and you can feel quite safe walking through the center day or night. To avoid pickpockets, be sure to keep you hands on your wallet or purse, and wear your backpack on your chest while traveling in trams and Metro cars.

Money/Currency

The **Czech crown** (Koruna) is the official currency of the Czech Republic. It is decimal-based and comes in bank notes of 50, 100, 200, 500, 1,000, 2,000 and 5,000 Kč; as well as coins of 1, 2, 5, 10, 20 and 50 Kč.

Currency Exchange

Banks are often the cheapest place to exchange your money for Czech crowns, offering the best exchange rates and a commission of just 2%. Although there are some good ones, the exchange

©Zdenek Pistek/iStockphoto

Czech currency

Comparing Prices

The cheapest things in Prague compared to other European cities are the food and beer *(see Must Eat and Nightlife)*. At most local pubs, you can buy a beer for around 25–40 Kč and a main course for around 120–200 Kč. Most electronic goods will cost the same if not slightly more than in other Western nations. Clothes and shoes also tend to cost slightly more than in other Western countries.

bureaus in Prague do not have a good reputation overall. Be sure you know how many Czech crowns to expect before handing over your cash, as the rates advertised in the window might not be what you get. Steer clear of anyone who offers to change money for you on the street; this is a scam to sell tourists counterfeit notes, which are not accepted as valid currency.

ATMs

ATMs are located throughout the city center. They will accept all internationally issued cards such as Visa and MasterCard. This is usually the easiest way to change money when traveling to Prague. Cash is dispensed in Czech crowns. Ask your local bank about any charges that might be incurred while using your card in Prague ATMs.

Credit Cards

Almost all the hotels and shops in the center of Prague accept credit and debit cards, but many restaurants and pubs do not. The most widely accepted cards are Visa and MasterCard. For lost or stolen credit cards, call the following local numbers.
American Express – 222 800 111
Diners Club – 267 314- 85
MasterCard/Eurocard –
261 354 650
Visa – 224-125-353

Travelers' Checks

Travelers' checks are generally not accepted in shops and restaurants. You can exchange your travelers' checks for cash at a bank for a commission of around 2%. Exchange offices also offer this service; they will charge between 3% and 10% commission, but the rates are sometimes slightly better.

Smoking

Smoking is permitted in most restaurants and bars, with some offering both smoking and non-smoking sections. Completely non-smoking restaurants are becoming more common, but are still definitely in the minority. The entrances to restaurants and bars are required by law to have a sticker identifying them as smoking or non-smoking establishments.

Street sign

©Prague Information Service

Important Phone Numbers	
Emergencies	☎ **112**
Police	☎ 158
City Police	☎ 156
Ambulance	☎ 155
Fire Department	☎ 150
Directory assistance in the Czech Republic	☎ 1180
Directory assistance for telephone numbers abroad	☎ 1181

Tipping

At some restaurants, particularly if you are dining in a group of six or more, a minimum service charge may be included; otherwise, leaving a tip of 10–15 percent is standard (*see Must Eat*). It is customary to give hotel bellhops 20 Kč per bag, and hotel chamber maids 20 Kč per night. Tip taxi drivers 5–10 percent of the fare.

Telephone

If you are staying in Prague for an extended period, consider purchasing a cell phone in the city. A phone with a SIM card and prepaid minutes will usually not cost more than 982 Kč /€40, depending on which operator you choose. The three main mobile-phone companies in the Czech Republic are **O2 Telefonica**, **Vodafone** and **T-Mobile**. Each one charges different rates for national and international calls. When **calling within the Czech Republic**, there are no area or city codes to dial in addition to the nine-digit number. Numbers beginning with 6 or 7 indicate a mobile phone. To **call abroad**, dial 00 + country code + national number of the line you're calling.

Touring Tip

Prague Information Service *(in Prague, call 12 444)* offers a help line available in Czech, English and German. It offers information on sightseeing, cultural events, public transport, and phone numbers and addresses of stores and services *(Mon–Fri 8am–7pm; local calling rates are charged)*.

Time Zone

Prague is in the Central European time zone, one hour ahead of Greenwich Mean Time and six hours ahead of New York City (EST). Daylight Saving Time (clocks advance one hour) goes into effect from spring through early fall.

Water

Prague's water is quite clean and is tested regularly, but you may prefer bottled water (available at hotel gift shops and convenience stores). Hotels often stock free bottled water for guests (check to make sure it is complimentary). Carrying bottled drinking water is a must when exploring Prague in the summer months, since the heat can quickly lead to dehydration.

PRACTICAL INFORMATION

THE GOLDEN CITY

Gone are the dark days of Kafkaesque dimly lit streets. Prague is now a vibrant city in the heart of Europe with a café culture and a shopping scene to rival those of many other European capitals. This city knows how to build bridges over history's troubled waters to affirm its identity. And whether you fancy historic sites or local beer – The Golden City's liquid gold – Prague really does have it all.

Beginnings of a Village

Located in the center of Bohemia, a region ringed by mountains, Prague is bisected by the Vltava River. Just north of Prague in the 9C, Přemyslid Prince Bořivoj I built Levý Hradec, a small castle on the river's left bank. Eventually, the princely dwelling was moved to the rocky outcropping that came to be called Hradčany (today's Castle Quarter). In the 10C, a merchant village developed at the foot of the castle on the cliff side. On the other bank, three roads led away from the river crossing; each one would eventually give rise to its own neighborhood.

The right bank developed rapidly. In the 11C, a market was already taking place at the site of present-day Old Town Square. The wooden bridge crossing the Vltava was replaced by the stone Judith Bridge (the predecessor to Charles Bridge) around 1170, and a web of streets began to take shape. Old Town (Staré Město) was granted city status around 1230; and as early as the mid-13C, it was surrounded by walls and defensive towers. The problem of floods was resolved by raising the ground level (thus all the vaulted cellars). In the 13C, the Jewish community of Josefov formed around the center of the Old Town, and the founding of Charles University in 1348 brought new life to Prague. After Otakar II revived the development of the left bank, the area took the name Menší Město pražské (Lesser Town of Prague), now Malá Strana, the Lesser Town. It wasn't until 1784 that the four Prague boroughs (Old Town, New Town, Castle Quarter and Lesser Town) were united.

Vltava River

©Prague Information Service

INTRODUCTION

Golden Age of Alchemy

No one seems to know the exact origin of Prague's nickname, The Golden City. Perhaps it refers to the golden domes of the capital's Baroque churches, or, more likely, it recalls the medieval practice of alchemy, the science of turning common minerals and base metals into gold. In the early 1600s, under the reign of Rudolf II, Prague attracted a melting pot of scientists, astronomers, artists and, in particular, alchemists. Famous alchemists who walked Prague's cobbled lanes include Englishmen Edward Kelley and John Dee. Another notable alchemist, perhaps better known for his work as an astronomer, was the Dane **Tycho Brahe** (1546–1601), who spent much of his life in Prague and is buried in the **Church of Our Lady Before Týn★★** *(see Religious Sites).*

Prague Rising

In the mid-14C, Emperor Charles IV changed the face of Prague. The spires of the Gothic cathedral of St. Vitus were raised over the Castle Quarter and a new bridge over the Vltava was built. During this time, the New Town was planned out, including enough space between its defensive walls to allow the expansion of the city to continue until modern times. Prague, then the residence of the Holy Roman Empire of the German Nation, was already one of the most beautiful cities in Europe.

The **Thirty Years' War** (1618–48) set Prague's development back significantly. As a result of their victories in the Czech lands, the **Hapsburgs** ruled here for 300 years following the war. Waves of German immigrants flowed into the city, and by the end of the 18C, Prague's Czech culture and language were waning.

Things started to look up during the **Czech National Revival** in the 19C, when Czech citizens came back to the city. As a result, working- and middle-class districts such as Smíchov, Žižkov and Vinohrady stretched beyond the city walls. Enormous buildings were constructed in choice locations: the **National Museum★** in 1890, the **National Theater★★★** in 1883, the **Rudolfinum★** in 1884, and the **Municipal House★★★** in 1911. All over the city, monuments were installed to remind the Czechs of their history and national identity; the **Statue of Saint Wenceslas★★** is the principal emblem among these.

The Capital City

Chosen as the capital of Czechoslovakia when the country was founded in 1918, Prague began to take on the appearance of a modern metropolis. Progressive architecture, such as the **Trade Fair Palace★★★**, took its place alongside the Functionalist buildings. Prague became known as the "Paris of the East" for its multicultural, cosmopolitan air, complete with cafés where writers would wax philosophical until dawn. These days of the **First Republic** were Prague's brightest for many years to come. The Germans took over in 1939, followed by the Soviets in 1948. For 40 years after that, Prague was hidden behind the dark Iron Curtain, but its cultural spirit lived on through its people, who privately kept their traditions alive.

The Dark Years

After WWII, the government deported more than 3.5 million German-speaking residents and Hungarians – including those who had fought against the Nazis. On February 25, 1948, the **Communist Party** seized power in what is known as the **Czech Coup**. Mass demonstrations and the fear of a massacre shook President Edvard Beneš, who allowed a Communist

government to form. Jan Masaryk, the only independent member of the government, was the victim of defenestration (he was thrown out a window). As a result, a surge of emigration began.

In 1952, the party secretary, Rudolf Slánský, himself responsible for a great number of political purges, was arrested along with 13 other Communist dignitaries accused of leading a "Trotskyite-Titoite-Zionist conspiracy." After a staged trial, 11 of the officials were sentenced to death, and many others were persecuted.

Prague Spring

In the 1960s, a process of de-Stalinization began. Victims of the staged hearings in the 1950s were absolved. The Slovak **Alexander Dubček** became General Secretary of the KSČ and promoted what he called "socialism with a human face." In April 1968, his reforms gave rise to a welcome period of political liberalization known as **Prague Spring**.

Spring was not to last. On August 21 of that year, 500,000 soldiers of the Warsaw Pact invaded

Soviet tanks line the street, August 28, 1968

©Bettmann/CORBIS

Czechoslovakia. "Normalization" purged the party of any mutineers, and repression was re-established. These measures caused a second wave of emigration. Only in the 1970s would dissidence be heard, through the publication of *samizdats* – clandestine pamphlets – and the creation of Charter 77.

The Velvet Revolution

The Velvet Revolution began with a candlelit march on November 17, 1989, shortly after the fall of the Berlin Wall. When participants of the march decided to change the course of their parade, the police reacted with violence, inciting the people's indignation.

Two days later, the Civic Forum, led by **Václav Havel**, was created to organize the forces of the opposition. Every day thereafter until the Communists left, thousands of demonstrators took turns supporting the forum. On December 29, Havel was elected president of the Republic. On January 1, 1993, Czechoslovakia officially split – in what is known as the "Velvet Divorce" – into the Czech Republic and Slovakia.

A 21st-Century City

Havel went on to serve the maximum two terms as a beloved president, and was replaced by the controversial former Prime Minister and vocal Euroskeptic, **Václav Klaus**, who staunchly believes man is not responsible for global warming. Even so, he presided over the country's accession to the European Union in 2004. While the Communist Party still garners some support among the populace, today's government is a tripartite center-right coalition.

Alexander Dubček with Václav Havel after the Velvet Revolution

©S. Lehman/age fotostock

Although the leading Civic Democratic (ODS) Party enjoyed the Czech Republic's EU presidency in 2009, that period might be better remembered for Prime Minister Miroslav Topolánek's naked appearance in poolside pictures at a party thrown by controversial Italian Prime Minister Silvio Berlusconi.

Today, debate rages about whether the country should join the Eurozone, with Euroskeptics like Klaus saying it was a good thing not to do, in light of the economic turmoil faced by many other Eurozone members. Politics aside, the capital and largest city of the Czech Republic retains an incomparable magic and a rich tradition of multiculturalism, fueled by the coexistence of Czech, German and Jewish cultures. Despite its turbulent past and current struggles, Prague thrives as a bustling cosmopolitan city – a unique and unforgettable place to discover.

NEIGHBORHOODS

The name Prague means "threshold" (*Praha* in Czech), and crossing between the city's main districts is in many ways like stepping into new worlds ripe for the discovering. Each neighborhood has a vibrant life and character shaped – physically in its streets and culturally in its personality – by its long and intertwined history. The Vltava River binds Prague together, and on its east bank sits **Old Town★★★**, **Jewish Town★★★** and New Town; on the west awaits **Lesser Town★★★** and the **Castle Quarter★★★**.

OLD TOWN★★★
(Staré Město)

Of Prague's many neighborhoods, it is Old Town that speaks the loudest of the city's past, and, indeed, it is the oldest of all of Prague's districts and comprised the entire medieval settlement. After Old Town became an official town in 1231, a fortification was built around it, complete with a crescent-shaped moat and a stone wall running the route that follows the modern streets Revoluční, **Na Příkopě★★** and **Národní★**. The moat and wall were dismantled soon after Charles IV founded the New Town in the 14C, and today only the **Powder Tower★** *(see Historic Sites)* remains as one of the fortification's original gates. Old Town is the heart and soul of

Prague, both in terms of its iconic sights and its vibrant cultural scene. You can easily spend an entire day (or more) wandering the winding, cobblestone alleyways of this area. For a magical experience, let yourself get a little lost; you're bound to discover a piece of history and a thing of beauty at every turn. Don't forget to look up at the top floors of the Renaissance houses and Baroque façades that you pass to admire the whimsical statues, skillfully crafted and preserved sgraffiti, and other lovely architectural details.

Old Town Square★★★
(Staroměstské náměstí)

Old Town is bordered on three sides by New Town, following the lines of the old fortification as it

Façade of the Sternberg Palace – National Gallery, Old Town

©Peter Erik Forsberg/age fotostock

MUST SEE

Jan Hus Memorial, Old Town Square

©Rod Purcell/Apa Publications

arcs along the Vltava River and surrounds the **Jewish Town★★★**. Hub of this neighborhood, Old Town Square *(see Historic Squares)* is crammed with so many Prague landmarks that it's hard to know where to look first; and from the bemused expressions on many visitors' faces there, this is not an uncommon dilemma.

The most recognizable features of Old Town Square are the Gothic spires of the **Church of Our Lady Before Týn★★** *(see Religious Sites)*. And in the center of the square, the steps of the **Jan Hus Memorial★★** *(see Monuments and Memorials)* are often crowded with tourists eager for a rest and locals chatting over a paper cup of take-out coffee.

To the north begins the ritzy **Pařížská třída★★** area, which marks the beginning of the Jewish Town. The **Astronomical Clock★★★** *(see Architectural Landmarks)* outside the **Old Town Hall★** *(see Historic Sites)* is one of Prague's most incredible sights, and the area right in front of it often brims with people awaiting the clock's hourly chiming show.

For a charming way to view Old Town, hop on to one of the **horse-drawn carriages** *(see Family Fun)* that stand close to the **Church of St. Nicholas★★** *(see Religious Sites)*, or head into the church to check out the daily free concert.

Karlova ulice★
(Charles Street)

If you follow the tourist hordes away from Old Town Square toward Charles Bridge, you will inevitably be swept along narrow, twisting Charles Street, which was originally built as three separate streets. Because of its proximity to

Old Town's Best Bites

Many of the city's most notable restaurants are located in the Old Town, including **La Dégustation Bohême Bourgeoise** and **Lokál** *(see Must Eat for both)*, among many others. Favorites can fill up very quickly, though, so make sure to call ahead and book a table to avoid disappointment.

NEIGHBORHOODS

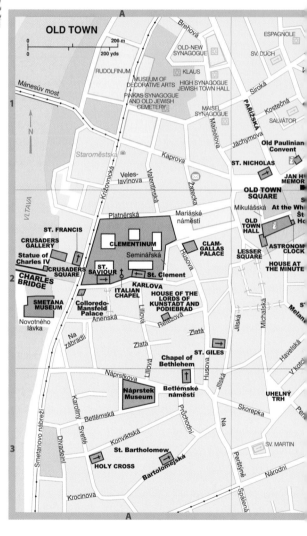

OLD TOWN

0 _____ 200 m
0 _____ 200 yds

Mánesův most

RUDOLFINUM

OLD-NEW SYNAGOGUE

KLAUS

ESPAGNOLE

SV. DUCH

MUSEUM OF DECORATIVE ARTS

HIGH SYNAGOGUE
JEWISH TOWN HALL

PINKAS SYNAGOGUE AND OLD JEWISH CEMETERY

Široká

PAŘÍŽSKÁ

Kostečná

SALVÁTOR

MAISEL SYNAGOGUE

Jáchymova

Old Paulinian Convent

Maiselova

ST. NICHOLAS

JAN H
MEMOR

Staroměstská

Kaprova

Velesla-vínova

Valentínská

Žatecká

OLD TOWN SQUARE

Mikulášská   At the Wh
Št
Ho

Platnéřská

Mariánské náměstí

OLD TOWN HALL

 i

VLTAVA

Křížovnická

ST. FRANCIS

Seminářská

CLEMENTINUM

CLAM-GALLAS PALACE

LESSER SQUARE

ASTRONOM
CLOCK

CRUSADERS GALLERY

Husova

HOUSE AT THE MINUTE

Statue of Charles IV

CRUSADERS SQUARE

ST. SAVIOUR

St. Clement

KARLOVA

CHARLES BRIDGE

SMETANA MUSEUM

Colloredo-Mansfeld Palace

ITALIAN CHAPEL

HOUSE OF THE LORDS OF KUNŠTÁT AND PODIEBRAD

Jilská

Michalská

Meta

Novotného lávka

Anenská

Řetězová

Na zábradlí

Zlatá

Zlatá

ST. GILES

Havelská

Lilíová

V kotci

Náprstkova

Chapel of Bethlehem

Husova

Jilská

UHELNÝ TRH

S

Smetanovo nábřeží

Karolíny

Náprstek Museum

Betlémské náměstí

Průchodní

Na

Skořepka

Pe

Betlémská

Divadelní

Světlé

Konviktská

SV. MARTIN

Perštýně

St. Bartholomew

HOLY CROSS

Bartolomějská

Perštýně

Národní

Spálená

Krocínova

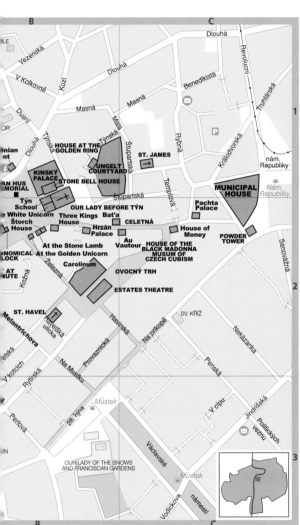

B

Dlouhá

Vězeňská

V Kolkovně

Kozí

Dlouhá

Benediktská

Revoluční

Truhlářská

Dušní

Masná

Masná

Malá

Štupartská

Rybná

Králodvorská

nám.
Republiky

inian
nt

HOUSE AT THE
GOLDEN RING

Týnská

Dlouhá

Týnská

ST. JAMES

UNGELT
COURTYARD

KINSKY
PALACE

STONE BELL HOUSE

**MUNICIPAL
HOUSE**

*Nám.
Republiky*

AN HUS
EMORIAL

OUR LADY BEFORE TÝN

Štupartská

Templová

Pachta
Palace

Týn
School

White Unicorn

Three Kings
House

Baťa

CELETNÁ

House of
Money

POWDER
TOWER

Senovážná

Štorch
House

Hrzán
Palace

NOMICAL
LOCK

At the Stone Lamb

Au
Vautour

HOUSE OF THE
BLACK MADONNA
MUSUM OF
CZECH CUBISM

AT
NUTE

At the Golden Unicorn

Carolinum

Koz ná

Železná

OVOCNÝ TRH

ST. HAVEL

Melantrichova

Havelská
ulička

Havířská

ESTATES THEATRE

SV. KŘÍŽ

Nekázanka

elská

V kotcích

Rytířská

Na Můstku

Provaznická

Na příkopě

Penská

V cípu

Jindřišská

Perlová

28. října

Můstek

Václavské

Politických
vězňů

OUR LADY OF THE SNOWS
AND FRANCISCAN GARDENS

Můstek

náměstí

Vodičkova

B

C

the **Clementinum★★** *(see Historic Sites)* – which was built by the Jesuits – it was known as Jesuit Street until 1848, when it was renamed. Once Charles Bridge was completed in the 14C, connecting the Old Town with the Lesser Town, Karlova became a busy thoroughfare. As you will see from the crowds peering into the souvenir shops that line this route today, not much has changed.

Ungelt Courtyard★

Behind the **Church of Our Lady Before Týn★★** lies the quaint Ungelt Courtyard (also called Týn courtyard or Týnský dvůr), which served in the 12C as a tax center, where merchants arriving from abroad would go to pay customs on their goods. The courtyard was originally separated by a moat of its own, to protect the merchants as they unloaded their goods. After falling into disrepair in the 20C, Ungelt was carefully restored in 1996. Today, it is home to several restaurants and shops, including a branch of the shop **Manufaktura** *(Melantrichova 17; see Shopping)*, as well as the gallery space in the **House at the Golden Ring★** *(see Museums)*. On one side of the courtyard, the **Ungelt Jazz Club** *(see Nightlife)* stages nightly concerts by stars of the local jazz scene.

Other Old Town Highlights

Other sights of note include the **Church of St. James★** *(see Religious Sites)* with its creepy legend, and the **Estates Theater** *(see Performing Arts)*, where Mozart premiered his opera *Don Giovanni* in 1787. And have no fear of going thirsty; there are pubs and cafes lurking in every nook and cranny of the Old Town. Though some tend to be overpriced tourist traps, there are just as many authentic places, some of which have been pouring beer – the country's national drink – for centuries.

Estates Theater

©Günter Lenz/age fotostock

Prague Castle

©Prague Information Service

CASTLE QUARTER★★★
(Hradčany)

Prague's Castle Quarter is a small but dense feast for the eyes. While several government ministries hold their offices in this area, it mainly consists of grand palaces and churches. Government offices are even housed in some of these spectacular structures. Situated on a hill atop the Lesser Town, the Castle Quarter affords magnificent views over the city. The neighborhood's small size belies the amount of things there are to see and do here, so it's worth dedicating at least half a day to exploring this part of the city. It wasn't until 1784 that the Castle Quarter officially joined the city of Prague; before that time, it had been an independent borough, like many other parts of Prague. As the district's main attractions,

Prague Castle★★★ *(see Palaces)* and **St. Vitus Cathedral★★★** *(see Religious Sites)* are visible from all along the Vltava River and are a postcard-perfect representation of the city. Indeed, the castle symbolizes the Czech state in more ways than one: Prague Castle is now the seat of the city's government, and the president himself has offices there.

Prague Castle★★★

One of the city's grandest sites, Prague Castle ranks as the largest castle complex in the world at 70,000m²/753,474sq ft. Within its complex, **St. Vitus Cathedral★★★** symbolizes the Czech nationhood, and between the two, there are countless rooms, chapels, galleries and exhibits to explore. While you're at the castle, be sure to watch the spectacle of

---

Leisure Time in New World

Near **Prague Castle★★★** is the beautiful **New World★★** (Nový Svět), a tourist-neglected stretch of seemingly untouched – but nicely touched-up – medieval and Renaissance houses along a leafy, cobbled street. Along that street, you'll find one of Prague's best restaurants, **U Zlaté studně** *(see Must Eat)*. It's also worth stopping by **U Černého vola** *(see Nightlife)*, a charming centuries-old pub that reeks (quite literally) of history.

NEIGHBORHOODS

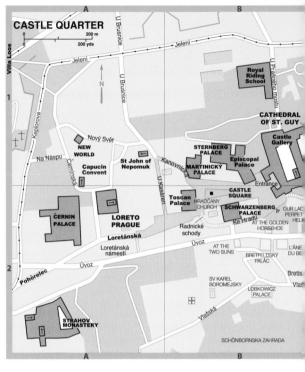

the changing of the guard.
After experiencing all of the
castle's grandeur, take a short
detour down **Golden Lane**★ *(see
Architectural Landmarks)*, a quaint
passage of narrow, candy-colored
medieval houses.

Castle Square★★★

The Castle Quarter revolves
around Castle Square *(see Historic
Squares)*, off of which you'll find
the gates to Prague Castle.
Stroll the square and admire the
Schwarzenberg Palace★, which
houses art from the National
Gallery, as well as the Italian
Renaissance-style **Archbishop's**

Palace *(see Palaces for both)*,
which to this day is the seat of
the Prague archbishop.
Among its many religious sites,
the Castle Quarter is home to the
Loreto Prague★★★ *(see Religious
Sites)*, which draws visitors from
near and far, both for its legendary
status as a "Santa casa," or Holy
House, as well as for its bells,
which chime an original score
composed by Antonin Dvořák.
Loretánská★★, the street that
climbs towards the Loreto Prague,
forms a little square adorned with
sophisticated **lampposts**.

Time Out in Josefov

While exploring the Jewish Town, there are plenty of restaurants and cafés where you can refuel. Within striking distance are **Les Moules** *(see Must Eat)*, a Belgian restaurant specializing in fresh imported mussels, and the **Hotel InterContinental** *(See Must Stay)*, which has a wonderful spa when you need to unwind *(see SPAS)*.

vestiges of its past. Between 1893 and 1913, the ghetto and its winding narrow streets were razed as part of an ambitious plan to make Prague look like Paris. Today only a handful of sites can testify to the area's heritage.

Pařížská třída ★★
(Paris Street)

Jewish Town centers on this central Parisian-style boulevard, fittingly called **Paris Street** *(see Shopping)*, a leafy stretch that runs from Old Town Square to the riverbank. It looks up at the **Metronome** *(see Architectural Landmarks)*, which was once the imposing site of a giant statue of Josef Stalin. Pařížská is Prague's Champs Élysées, lined with boutique after designer boutique (think Prada, Gucci, Burberry) and high-end restaurants and cafés. Once you step off the showy sidewalk and turn down a side street, you'll catch glimpses of the Jewish Town's past. The famed German-speaking writer **Franz Kafka** was born in this quarter, and his childhood home is now open as the **Franz Kafka Museum** *(see Museums)*. A **statue★** *(see*

JEWISH TOWN★★★
(Josefov)

Prague's Jewish Town, also called the Jewish Quarter, is the smallest district in the city. Jewish immigrants began settling here in the 10C, and after a pogrom was established in 1096, the area was walled off as a ghetto. On Easter Sunday 1389, more than 1,500 Jews murdered in one of the worst pogroms. The walled ghetto had its heyday in the 16C, around the time that, according to legend, the mythical creature **Golem** was created *(see sidebar, p 68)*. Enveloped by Old Town on all sides, Jewish Town bears few

NEIGHBORHOODS

43

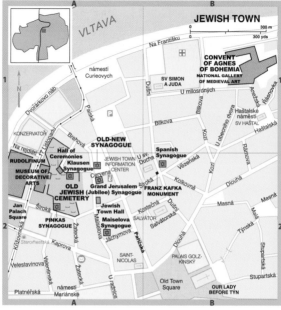

The map shows "JEWISH TOWN" with streets and landmarks including VLTAVA, Na Františku, CONVENT OF AGNES OF BOHEMIA NATIONAL GALLERY OF MEDIEVAL ART, náměstí Curieovych, SV SIMON A JUDA, U milosrdných, KONZERVATOR, OLD-NEW SYNAGOGUE, Hall of Ceremonies, RUDOLFINUM, Klausen Synagogue, JEWISH TOWN INFORMATION CENTER, Spanish Synagogue, SV HAŠTAL, Haštalské náměstí, MUSEUM OF DECORATIVE ARTS, Grand Jerusalem (Jubilee) Synagogue, FRANZ KAFKA MONUMENT, OLD JEWISH CEMETERY, Jan Palach Square, PINKAS SYNAGOGUE, Jewish Town Hall, Maiselova Synagogue, SAINT-NICOLAS, PALAIS GOLZ-KINSKY, Old Town Square, OUR LADY BEFORE TÝN.

Monuments and Memorials) of the writer occupies a place of prominence at the corner of Dušní and Vězeňská streets.

Old-New Synagogue

©Prague Information Service

Synagogues of Josefov

See Religious Sites for more details about the following synagogues mentioned in **bold**.

When the ghetto gave way to Prague's version of Paris, only six synagogues were left standing. The oldest still-functioning synagogue in Europe is the iconic **Old-New Synagogue★★★**, which dates to 1270 and still holds regular services. Next to it is the **Jewish Town Hall** *(see Historic Sites)*, with its Hebrew clock. In the **Maisel Synagogue,** you'll find an extensive collection of Jewish artifacts from Central Europe, amassed by the Nazis.

The **Spanish Synagogue** dates to the 19C and is named for its striking Moorish architecture, while the **Pinkas Synagogue★★** houses a moving list of the names

Lesser Town

of every single local Jewish person rounded up in the Holocaust – numbering almost 80,000. The Pinkas Synagogue also serves as the entrance to the hauntingly lovely **Old Jewish Cemetery★★★** *(see Historic Sites)* with its mass of jumbled gravestones. If you're pressed for time and can't tour the cemetery, the café in the nearby **Museum of Decorative Arts★** *(see Museums)* offers a good look over the headstones through the café's windows.

LESSER TOWN★★★
(Malá Strana)

The most common translations of Malá Strana as the "Lesser Town" hardly do it justice, as the Czech word *malá* in this context translates as "smaller" and actually refers to the district's position on the west side of the river. Indeed, Prague's Left Bank is a rich component of the city's historic center, a crucial part both in history and layout that has made Prague into the unforgettable whole it is today.

Lesser Town has a distinctly different feel than that of Old Town. Its cobbled paths slant up toward the Castle Quarter and the houses appear smaller and more exaggerated, as in a fairy tale. There are ornate palaces at many turns, a testament to the city's beginnings as a medieval village settled by Germans. Old Town, on the other hand (and on the other side of the river), was populated by wealthy Czechs. In 1257 the Lesser Town was formed, with several existing settlements united under the name the Lesser Town of Prague (Malé Město Pražské). Under the reign of Otakar II, the district gained status as a royal town, thus allowing it more funds and privileges.

You'll sense the magical air of Lesser Town, its colorful façades and quaint alleyways – some so narrow that you must enter single-file (such as the darling passageway leading from Cihelná

Touring Tip

If you cross **Charles Bridge★★★** early in the morning or late at night, there's a good chance you might just have the whole span to yourself, making for some incredible photo opportunities.

NEIGHBORHOODS

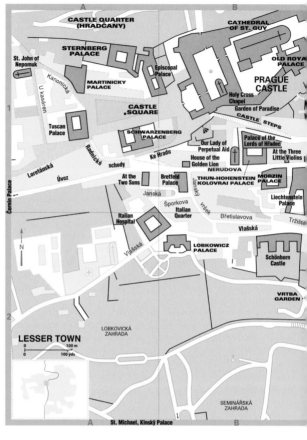

street down to the river, where a
tiny traffic light gives you the go-
ahead) – crammed full of artisans'
shops and galleries, cellar cafés
and wine bars, and historic pubs
and beer halls.

Charles Bridge★★★

Well worth pushing through the
crowds to see, Charles Bridge
(see Architectural Landmarks) is
the ideal direction from which to
approach the Lesser Town and to

appreciate its beauty. Strolling
across the bridge that spans the
Vltava River from Old Town to
Lesser Town gives you idyllic views
of the hilly left bank, with the
leafy **Petřín Hill** *(see Parks and
Gardens)* rising on the left and the
magnificent Prague Castle – with
the striking St. Vitus Cathedral
poking out from amid the castle
complex – on the right. After
admiring the views and the statues
that line the bridge, the **Lesser**

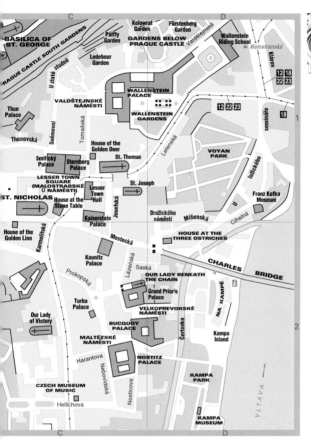

BASILICA OF ST. GEORGE

PRAGUE CASTLE SOUTH GARDENS

U zlaté studně

Pálffy Garden

Kolowrat Garden

Fürstenberg Garden

GARDENS BELOW PRAGUE CASTLE

Ledebour Garden

Valdštejnská

Wallenstein Riding School

Malostranská

Klárov

12 18
22 23

WALLENSTEIN PALACE

Thun Palace

VALDŠTEJNSKÉ NÁMĚSTÍ

Sněmovní

Tomášská

12 22 23

Thunovská

Letenská

WALLENSTEIN GARDENS

18

semináře

House of the Golden Deer

St. Thomas

VOYAN PARK

Směřický Palace

Sternberg Palace

LESSER TOWN SQUARE (MALOSTRANSKÉ U NÁMĚSTÍ)

Lesser Town Hall

St. Joseph

Josefská

Dražického náměstí

Míšenská

Cihelná

U lužického

Franz Kafka Museum

ST. NICHOLAS

House at the Stone Table

Kaiserstein Palace

House of the Golden Lion

Karmelitská

Mostecká

Lázeňská

Saská

HOUSE AT THE THREE OSTRICHES

CHARLES BRIDGE

Kaunitz Palace

Prokopská

OUR LADY BENEATH THE CHAIN

Turba Palace

Grand Prior's Palace

VELKOPŘEVORSKÉ NÁMĚSTÍ

Our Lady of Victory

BUCQUOY PALACE

Čertovka

NA KAMPĚ

i

Kampa Island

MALTÉZSKÉ NÁMĚSTÍ

Harantova

NOSTITZ PALACE

Nebovidská

Nosticova

KAMPA PARK

VLTAVA

CZECH MUSEUM OF MUSIC

Hellichova

KAMPA MUSEUM

Charles Bridge

©Prague Information Service

A Day in the Park

Go to the left after crossing Charles Bridge, and you'll come to
Kampa Park★ *(see Parks and Gardens)*. This lush, riverside island is home
to several top-notch eateries like **Kampa Park** restaurant, the flagship of a
renowned hospitality group that also owns the nearby **Cowboys** steakhouse
and **Hergetova Cihelna** *(see Must Eat for all three)*. In nice weather, the
park functions as an open-air gallery space, sometimes taking to Kampa
Square for sidewalk exhibits; or going indoors at the **Jan and Meda Mládek
Foundation★★** *(see Museums)*, which houses an exhibit of Czech art.

Town Bridge Tower *(see Historic
Sites)* beckons you to make a grand
entrance into Lesser Town.

Over the Bridge

Immediately upon passing
through the bridge tower, you may
be spoiled for choice as to where
to go from the pretty **Mostecká**
(Bridge Street). Heading to the
right from Charles Bridge, duck
in to see the **House at the Three
Ostriches★** *(see Historic Sites)*, a
restaurant and hotel that was one
of Prague's first cafés.

If you have time, Lesser Town
is worth dedicating a day to
exploring. Start with the most
prominently identifiable feature,

the **Church of St. Nicholas★★★**
(see Religious Sites) on **Lesser
Town Square★** *(see Historic
Squares)*, long the marketplace hub
of the Lesser Town. Take in more
modern history on the square at
the recently renovated cultural
complex **Malostranská beseda**
(see Performing Arts), where you
can experience the creativity
that thrived here against all odds
throughout the 20C.

Garden Delights

Before huffing and puffing your
way up **Nerudova★★**, the busy
main pedestrian thoroughfare
leading from Charles Bridge up to
the Castle Quarter, Lesser Town's

Wallenstein Gardens

©Pavlo Maydikov/iStockphoto.com

Powder Tower and Municipal House

©Prague Information Service

many gardens are worth seeking out. With its weeping willows and fruit-laden trees, **Wallenstein Gardens★★** is a particularly lovely urban oasis. If you're yearning for longer strides than a walled-in garden can afford, head to **Petřín Park** *(see Parks and Gardens for both)*. Here you'll be rewarded with sweeping views over the city and options for several unique activities, such as climbing **Petřín Tower** and walking through the **Mirror Maze** *(see Family Fun for both)*.

NEW TOWN
(Nové Město)

Calling Nové Město the "new town" is relative, as its founding dates back to 1348, but out of all the Prague districts, it is the youngest. Faced with a rising population problem as well as the hankering to celebrate his coronation in a new city, King Charles founded the New Town as an independent royal city. He also moved the noisier and dirtier of the medieval trades out of the Old Town and into the New. Covering an area of 250ha/

617 acres, New Town is vast and varied. At **Republic Square** *(see Historic Squares)*, on the border of the Old and New Towns where the **Municipal House★★★** *(see Architectural Landmarks)* presides in its Secessionist and Art Nouveau grandeur over the crowds, the **Powder Tower** *(see Historic Sites)* stands as the last part of the original fortification – a moat and a wall – that once surrounded the Old Town. Sharing the square are the recently refurbished **Hybernia**

Trains in Transition

Prague's 1909 main train station, **Hlavní nádraží★** *(Wilsonova 8)*, is also in New Town, close to Wenceslas Square and the **State Opera** *(see Performing Arts)*. Currently undergoing a long-term reconstruction, the station is half modern and half Old World faded beauty. Seek out the lovely **Fantova atrium** and the **Fantova Café**, both named for prominent Czech Art Nouveau architect Josef Fanta.

NEIGHBORHOODS

NEW TOWN

0   200 m
0   200 yds

Maiselova · Široká · Vězeňská · Masna · Rybná · Truhlářská

Kaprova · Pařížská · Dlouhá · Kinský Palace · Králodvorská · Republic Square

Old Town Square · Železná · Štupartská · **PRAGUE CITY SAVINGS BANK** · Senovážná

KLEMENTINUM · **Carolinum** · **Myslbek** · **Prague**

Charles Bridge · Karlova · **Vernier Palace** · **Holy Cross** · TO JINDŘIŠ

Anenská · Havelská · **Commerce Bank** · Rytířská · Můstek · 28 října · **Mucha Mus**

Náprstkova · Betlémská · Skořepka · **House at the Black**

Konviktská · Perštýn · **OUR LADY OF THE SNOWS BASILICA** · **Ambassador** · **Golden Goose** · **Ph. Adam** · **Peterka House** · Politických · vězňů · **Main Post Office**

Karoliny · Světlé · Bartolomějská · Národní Třída · **ADRIA PALACE** · **GRAND HOTEL EVROPA**

Shooters Island · **Café Slava** · **SECESSIONIST BUILDINGS** · Národní Třída · **FRANCISCAN GARDEN** · Palackého · **MORAVIAN BANK** · Jalta H

Legionnaire's Bridge · Národní třída · **Baroque Palace** · **ST. URSULA** · Ostrovní · **MAGASIN NOVÁK**

NATIONAL THEATER · V jirchářích · Jungmannova · **WENCESLAS SQUARE (VÁCLAVSKÉ NÁMĚS**

QUAI MASARYK · Spálená · Vodičkova · Štěpánská · Ve Smečkách · Mezibranská

SLAVIC ISLAND · Pštrossova · Křemencova · Černá · Myslíkova · **NEW TOWN HALL** · Rezická · Žitná

Dětský ostrov · Na Zbořenci · Žitná · **CHARLES SQUARE** · MALÁ ŠTĚPÁNSKÁ · Na Hálkova

Náplavní · Na Zderaze · Zbořenci · **Sts. Cyril and Methodius** · Resslova · Lipová · Rybníčku

Alois-Jirásek Bridge · **ST. IGNATIUS** · Ječná · I. P. Pavlova

DANCING HOUSE · Trojanova · Salmovská · Kateřinská · **DVOŘÁK MUSEUM**

Karlovo náměstí · **SQUARE** · U nemocnice · Viničná · Sokolská · Na bojišti · Ke Karlovu

Commercial Bank of Czechoslovakia .... **B**
Bat'a. .... **D**
Wiehl House .... **E**
Museum of Communism .... **M**
Alfa Palace .... **N**
Koruna Palace .... **Q**
Silva-Tarouca Palace .... **R**
Statue of St. Wenceslas .... **S**

EMMAUS CONVENT · **ST. JOHN ON THE ROCK** · Vyšehradská · Benátská · Apolinářská

Faust House · Kateřinská

Czech Police Museum

Theater *(see Performing Arts)* and the glitzy **Palladium mall** *(see sidebar, p123).*

Wenceslas Square★★★

New Town embraces the borders of Old Town, hugging it along the streets Revoluční, **Na Příkopě★★** ("On The Moat") and **Národní třída★** (National Avenue), where you'll find the highest

concentration of attractions. However, even the outlying parts of the district have much to offer, both in terms of historic sights as well as some of the city's best dining and nightlife options. The defining feature of New Town, Wenceslas Square *(see Historic Squares)* is a grand park that has served for centuries as a market-place and central meeting point.

Wenceslas Square

©Prague Information Service

Charles Square and Beyond

The largest square in the country, **Charles Square★** *(see Historic Squares)* is home to the **New Town Hall★** *(see Historic Sites)*.

It's a short walk from the square down to the Vltava River, where you can admire the striking design of the **Dancing House★★** *(see Architectural Landmarks)*, enjoy a stroll along the embankment, and pick out a restaurant to sample – such as **Botel Matylda** *(see Must Eat)*, set on a small boat overlooking Prague Castle.

New Town borders Vyšehrad, where the **Church of Sts. Peter and Paul★** *(see Religious Sites)* and the **Vyšehrad Gardens** *(see Parks and Gardens)* are protected to this day by the remains of the 18C **Vyšehrad Fortress★** *(see Historic Sites)*.

Here you can visit the **National Museum★** *(see Museums)* and hop into shops including **Neo Luxor** *(Václavské náměstí 41; www.neoluxor.cz)*, the largest bookstore in Central Europe. Here, in addition to thousands of other books, you'll find maps and travel guides in English (and other languages).

NEIGHBORHOODS

HISTORIC SQUARES

All throughout history, the main square of any town or city – no matter how humble or grand – has been the meeting place of the community, the focal point for festivities, and, in times of turmoil, a central spot for political rallies. Prague's many neighborhoods each have such squares, which, if you're fortunate enough to turn the right corner and stumble upon, can be the perfect spot to perch on a fountain's edge or at an outdoor café and gather your thoughts. Many of the sites in **bold** are described elsewhere in the guide; check Index for page numbers.

Old Town Square★★★
(Staroměstske naměsti)

Bounded by Dlouhá and Celetná Sts., Old Town.
Metro A: Staroměstská.

You haven't properly seen Prague without a stroll around Old Town Square, and you can easily dedicate several hours to exploring all that the storied cobbled expanse has to offer. Crowds gather to watch the whimsical 600-year-old **Astronomical Clock★★★** chime the hour, and, above that, the rooftop of the tower at **Old Town Hall★** affords stunning views over the maze of red rooftops and winding alleyways. The square's centerpiece, the **Jan Hus Memorial★★** depicts the martyred religious leader, while the spires of **St. Nicholas Church★★** and **Our Lady Before Týn★★** rise above the plaza. Fill up on the eye candy that is the Baroque, Renaissance and Rococco façades surrounding the square, such as the intricately painted **Štorch House★★** at No. 16.

Wenceslas Square★★★
(Václavské náměstí)

Bounded by Na Příkopě and Wilsonova Sts., New Town.
Metro A: Můstek; or A, B: Muzeum.

Home to revolutionary and commercial evolution alike, Wenceslas Square stretches from the busy pedestrian intersection of Můstek past flower beds and sausage stands up to where the **National Museum★** presides over the equestrian **Statue of St. Wenceslas★★** – now a popular

The Main Events

Old Town Square★★★ has enough going for it to draw crowds any day of the year, but during the **Christmas Markets** *(see Calendar of Events)* in December and the **Easter Markets** in early spring, the square is more crowded than ever. For these events, the cobblestone plaza fills with sausage and beer stands and wooden stalls selling Czech-made crafts. The lighting of the Christmas tree on the first day of the Christmas Market is the busiest time. On **New Year's Eve**, the square turns raucous with fireworks displays and concerts. And when the Czech team makes it to an **ice-hockey championship game**, expect the square to hold a big screen and a commensurate number of fans.

MUST SEE

meeting point. Dating to 1348, the long square was envisioned by King Charles IV as an open marketplace in his plan for New Town. Nowadays, it seems that nearly every building has been taken over by glitzy jewelry shops and clothing-store chains, but if you look up, many of the preserved façades display detailed frescoes or sgraffito.

For more on the buildings bordering Wenceslas Square, see Architectural Landmarks.

Castle Square★★
(Hradčanské náměstí)

Bounded by Lorentánská St. and the Castle Steps, Hradčany. Tram 22: Pražský hrad.

This vast expanse is one of Prague's grandest, a fitting entrance to **Prague Castle★★★**.
Make sure to catch the changing of the guards at the gates, which takes place on the hour from 5am to 11pm, with a fanfare at noon. Bordered by the **Archbishop's Palace** and **Schwarzenberg Palace★**, the square features spectacular views over the city, and marks the beginning of **New World★★** (*see sidebar, p 41*) and the **Castle Steps**.

Crusaders' Square★★
(Křižovnické náměstí)

Bounded by Křižovnická and Karlova Sts., Old Town. Metro A: Staroměstská.

The gateway to **Charles Bridge★★★** from Old Town, this square is Prague's smallest, featuring the church of **St. Salvator★**, part of the **Clementinum★★**. Note the statue of King Charles IV in the center, the ornate entrance to the monastery that includes the **Church of St. Francis★★**. Impossible to miss, the arch of the **Old Town Bridge Tower★★** forms the entrance to the iconic bridge.

©Chmura Frank/age fotostock

New World

HISTORIC SQUARES

Grand Priory Square★★
(Velkopřevorské náměstí)

Bounded by Lázeňská and Hroznová Sts., Lesser Town. Trams 12, 20 or 22: Hellichova.

While this landscaped square, located between Charles Bridge and **Kampa Park★**, has several notable buildings, such as the **Grand Priory Palace** (Velkopřevorský palác), its biggest draw is probably the **Lennon Wall** (*see sidebar, p 59*). The **Grand Priory Mill** (Velkopřevorský mlýn) dates to the 13C, and its wooden water wheel gives a feel for this area in centuries past.

The railings of the bridge crossing to this square are covered with engraved locks; tradition dictates that newlyweds attach a symbol of their love here.

Maltese Square★★
(Maltézské náměstí)

Bounded by Prokopská and Lázeňská Sts., Lesser Town. Trams 12, 20 or 22: Hellichova.

The name of the square, which played a role in Miloš Forman's 1984 Academy Award-winning film *Amadeus*, recalls the presence of the Knights of the Maltese Cross in this area of Malá Strana. The enclave of the supreme order of Crusaders (then known as the Knights of St. John, whose statue stands at the north end of the square) was established in 1169 near the entrance to the bridge. Ringed by cozy restaurants and cafés, Maltese Square is also the home of **Nostitz Palace★** and **Turba Palace**.

Charles Square★
(Karlovo náměstí)

Bounded by Na Moráni and Žitná Sts., New Town. Metro B: Karlovo náměstí.

At 8.5ha/21 acres, Charles Square is the largest in the Czech Republic, and one of the largest in Europe. Initially a livestock market, it was built in the mid-14C as a vital part of King Charles IV's New Town. Today, the square is divided into two parks centered on fountains, where people gather to picnic or relax on the grass. At the northern end lies the **New Town Hall★**.

Lesser Town Square★
(Malostranské náměstí)

Bounded by Nerudova and Mostecká Sts., Lesser Town. Trams 12, 20 or 22: Malostranské náměstí.

Grand Priory Mill

©Mark Beton/age fotostock

The veritable hub of Malá Strana since the 10C, Malostranské náměstí is divided into an upper and a lower half; the upper part includes the **Church of St. Nicholas★★★**, and the lower half focuses on the cultural center of **Malostranská beseda**, which houses a restaurant, café, bar and music venue. Smiřicky Palace, at No. 18, played a crucial role in kicking off the Thirty Years' War.

Malostranská beseda, Lesser Town Square
©Martin Kralovsky/Malostranska beseda

Small Square★
(Malé náměstí)

Bounded by Karlova and U Radnice Sts., Old Town. Metro A: Staroměstská.

True to its name, this triangular square is much smaller than nearby Old Town Square, but it's worth a gander for its historic houses as well as Prague's oldest fountain, encased by wrought-iron lattice and topped with gilt figures of an angel and a lion. Built between 1876 and 1878, the fountain was disconnected in the 1990s.

Palacký Square
(Palackého náměstí)

Bounded by Na Moráni St. and Rašínovo nábřeží, New Town. Metro B: Karlovo náměstí.

With the Vltava River on one side and the reconstructed **Emauzy Monastery** on the other, this open cobblestone square on the edge of New Town has a pretty park area and a statue to 19C historian **František Palacký** in its center. The square's reputation as "Prague's Hyde Park," where people can protest freely without city approval, makes it a popular place for political rallies.

Peace Square
(Náměstí Míru)

Bounded by Anglická and Francouzská Sts., Vinohrady. Metro A: Náměstí Míru.

Just a few blocks southeast of Wenceslas Square, the hip residential neighborhood of Vinohrady begins at this square, which features the impressive neo-Gothic **Church of St. Ludmila** and the **Vinohrady Theater** (which you may recognize from the 2010 film *The Illusionist*).

Republic Square
(Náměstí Republiky)

Bounded by Revoluční and V Celnici Sts., Old Town. Metro B: Náměstí Republiky.

The focal points of this square, which borders Old Town and New Town, are the Gothic Powder Tower, which marks the beginning of the **Royal Route**, and the grand Secessionist **Municipal House★★★**. Facing this is the reconstructed **Hybernia Theater**, as well as the **Kotva** and **Palladium** shopping centers *(see Shopping)*.

PALACES

The palaces, castles and chateaus of Prague dot the capital cityscape like grand dames at a ball, and to explore their rich cultural and historical heritage is to discover Prague. Walk the very same corridors as storied leaders, listen to the echoes of balls and banquets in great halls, and wonder at the skill that went into the construction of these fortresses and stately manors. Even though not all of Prague's palaces are open to the public, they can all be admired at least from the outside.

Prague Castle★★★
(Pražský Hrad)

Hradčanské náměstí, Hradčany. Tram 22: Pražský hrad. Castle complex open year-round daily 5am–midnight.Gardens open year-round daily at 10am; closing hours vary by season. Interior open Apr–Oct 9am–6pm, Nov–Mar 9am–4pm. Closed Dec. 24. Short tour (includes sights described below) 250 Kč. Long tour (includes additional exhibits and buildings) 350 Kč. 224 373 368. www.hrad.cz.

At 70,000m²/753,474sq ft, Prague Castle is the biggest castle complex in the world. This landmark is one of the city's most visible sights, be it from along the Vltava River or up on Petřín Hill. It was built around the year 880 by Prince Bořivoj of the Premyslid Dynasty and comprises a series of courtyards, church buildings and stately offices where you can happily wander for most of a day. The castle is both the seat of the current government (the president's offices and ceremonial halls are squirreled away in the labyrinthine buildings, some of which date to the 10C) as well as the symbolic representation of the nation's turbulent past. The marvelous **Story of Prague Castle exhibit★★** *(in the cellar of the Old Royal Palace; same hours as Prague Castle;140 Kč)* describes the castle's history.

Focal point of the complex, the soaring Gothic **St. Vitus Cathedral★★★** *(see Religious*

Prague Castle

©Prague Information Service

The Ballroom

In the **Royal Gardens**★★ *(see Parks and Gardens)* of Prague Castle, between the castle complex and the **Belvedere Summer Palace**★★, stands one of the city's most beautiful buildings, **Míčovna**★, or the Ballroom, which dates to the mid-16C. Though the inside is closed to the public, the outside is stunning in its beauty. Míčovna's detailed facade was painstakingly restored by the Communists in the 1950s – look for the sgraffito version of the hammer and sickle – after being severely damaged in World War II. The Ballroom was opened again in 1989 for private functions and occasional exhibitions.

Sites) dates to the 14C. The **Old Royal Palace**★★★ in the castle's Third Courtyard was once the seat of Bohemian princes, and its vast Vladislav Hall, once used for coronations and balls in medieval times, is now used for state ceremonies. **Basilica of St. George** ★★, along with its adjacent convent, is the second-oldest church in Prague. Though this structure dates to the early 10C, the exteriors feature Gothic renovations, and the basilica hosts rotating art exhibits and occasional concerts. **Golden Lane**★ *(see Architectural Landmarks)*, the entrance to which is accessible from within the castle walls, provides a magical glimpse of 14C Prague.

Adria Palace★★
(Palác Adria)

Corner of Národní třída & Jungmannova Sts., New Town. Metro B: Můstek. Not open to the public.

Built between 1922 and 1924, this extraordinary building is considered a masterpiece of the **Rondo Cubist style**, unique to Czechoslovakia and characterized by decorative flourishes on the façade. The palace houses the Art Nouveau-style **Caffe Adria**, whose walls bear photographs of movies that have been filmed in the building. Though the palace itself is not open to the public, the café's terrace affords a great view of the palace façade.

Belvedere Summer Palace★★
(Belveder Královský letohrádek)

*Mariánské hradby 1, **Hradčany**. Tram 22: Královský letohrádek. Open Apr-Oct 9am–5pm; times vary in winter. Closed Dec. 24. Visit by guided tour only: 30min 160 Kč; 1hr 240 Kč. 224 373 368 or 224 372 423. www.hrad.cz.*

The Belvedere, also known as the Royal Summer Palace, was built between 1537 and 1563 by Ferdinand I in the Italian Renaissance style, as a gift to his wife, Queen Anne.
The roof resembles the shape of an overturned boat's hull, and the walls are covered in reliefs depicting various scenes, including one of Ferdinand presenting a flower to Anne.
The palace affords a beautiful view of the **Belvedere Summer Palace gardens** and Prague Castle. Check out the garden's unique and charming **Singing Fountain** *(see sidebar, p58)*.

The Singing Fountain

If you listen closely enough, the fountain that sits in the garden of the **Belvedere Summer Palace★★** *(see p57)* has a song of the ages to sing. Known as **The Singing Fountain★** (Zpívající fontána), the two-tiered structure, wrought of copper and tin and placed prominently in the manicured gardens, was completed in 1568. Whimsically decorated with mythical animals and humans, the fountain spouts water from the creatures' mouths, and the sound that it makes when it comes into contact with the unusually thin metal below sounds like singing.

Troja Chateau★★
(Trojský zámek)

U Trojeského zámku 1, Troja. Metro C: Holešovice, and bus 112 to Zoologická zahrada. Open Apr–Oct Tue–Sun 10am–6pm, Nov–Mar Sat–Sun 10am–5pm. 120 Kč. 233 320 235. www.citygalleryprague.cz.

This Baroque palace, located north of the city center near the **Prague Zoo** *(see Family Fun)*, was originally built for Count Sternberg by French architect **Jean-Baptiste Mathey**. Sternberg ordered that the work begin in 1679, and that his chateau be built facing Prague Castle. Arriving by foot from the banks of the Vltava through the terrace gardens and climbing the monumental staircase to the front entrance, you get an idea of the luxury with which the count

sought to impress the monarch. The symmetrical palace takes its inspiration from new concepts by the Italian architects Fontana and Bernini. The monumental central part – including two levels of windows – is entirely taken up by the **ceremonial hall★★★**. Here, you'll note the remarkable use of space, thanks to trompe-l'oeil effects. Wings on both sides are flanked by corner pavilions with the two towers rising majestically above. The main axis of the building is longer on the north side, where the stables adjoin the horseshoe-shaped **grand staircase**, the only direct access from the ground floor to the ceremonial hall. To enhance the dimensions of the palace, Mathey set up a row of colossal red pilasters, utilizing the same color he used for the cornices and window frames. Much of the inside of the chateau is associated with the City Gallery of Prague, and contains a collection of **19C Czech paintings**.

Buquoy Palace★
(Buquoyský palác)

Velkopřevorské náměstí 2, Lesser Town. Trams 12, 20 or 2: Hellichova.

This particular site was designated by King Vladislav II as a hospital and church in the 12C, before

Troja Chateau

©Prague Information Service

being transformed in 1736 into a palace by connecting three neighboring houses. The palace, a typical example of Baroque architecture, has housed the French Embassy since 1919.

Clam-Gallas Palace★
(Clam-Gallasův palác)

Husova 20, Old Town. Metro A: Staroměstská. Open Tue–Sun 10am–6pm. Admission depends on exhibit; usually 50 Kč–100 Kč. 236 002 068 or 224 816 233.

This grand palace, an example of pure Viennese Baroque style, was conceived by **Bernhard Fischer von Erlach** and constructed by Italian architect Domenico Canevale in 1713 for Johann Wenceslas, Count of Gallas and Viceroy of Naples. The architect hired the greatest Prague-based sculptor at the time, **Mathias Bernard Braun**, to adorn the façade with statues, including the two pairs of giants supporting the twin porticoes. Mozart and his wife attended a ball at Clam-Gallas, and Beethoven once played a concert here. Today, it is home to the city's archives and the **Czech Museum of Fine Arts** *(see Museums)*.

Martinický Palace★
(Martinický palác)

Hradčanské náměstí 8, Hradčany. Tram 22: Pražský hrad. Opening hours vary. Call ahead for group tour (1–5 people). 100 Kč. 777 798 040. martinickypalac.cz.

A UNESCO-protected landmark, this palace sits across from Prague Castle on Castle Square. It exemplifies the Renaissance style and dates to the 16C, replacing a series of Gothic houses that once stood here. The palace, which changed hands many times, saw its heyday at the turn of the 20C, when as many as 70 families called Martinicky Palace home. In the 1950s, reconstruction work began to restore the residence to its former glory.

Schwarzenberg Palace★
(Schwarzenberský palace)

Hradčanské náměstí 2, Hradčany. Tram 22: Pražský hrad. Open year-round Tue–Sun 10am–6pm. 150 Kč. 233 081 716.

Now under the auspices of the National Gallery, this is arguably the most beautiful Renaissance building in Prague – as difficult as

---

The Lennon Wall

Despite having never visited Prague while alive, former Beatle **John Lennon** (1940–1980) has a personal legacy in the city's psyche. Students viewed his untimely death as a symbol of all that was wrong with the world, and, risking severe recrimination from the Communist authorities of the time, began painting a wall in Lesser Town with lyrics from Beatles songs in tribute. Under the cover of night, young people would come to scrawl personal messages of hope, love and peace, as well as comments against the regime. Despite rigorous police attempts to whitewash the wall, new inscriptions appeared daily. The wall remains today on Grand Priory Square as a symbol of youth and a tribute to those who heralded hope during the nation's dark times.

PALACES

it is to pick favorites. It was built between1545 and1563 by the architect Agostino Galli, and its façade is decorated with diamond-tipped bossage (uncut stone that projects from the building) and Venetian-style black-and-white sgraffiti.

Wallenstein Palace★
(Valdštejnský palác)

Valdštejnské náměstí 4, Lesser Town. Trams 12, 20 or 22: Malostranské náměstí. Open year-round Sat–Sun 10am–4pm.

At the foot of Prague Castle, this Baroque palace currently houses the Czech Senate as well as National Gallery exhibits. It comprises more than 20 original buildings, set about with courtyards and gardens. Wallenstein Palace, which dates to the end of the 17C, was designed by three Italian architects in a late Renaissance style for the wealthy general Albrecht von Wallenstein. General Wallenstein commanded the empire's armies and lived in the palace for only a

year before he was assassinated by King Ferdinand II. The palace is complemented by the surrounding **Wallenstein Gardens★★** *(see Parks and Gardens).*

Archbishop's Palace
(Arcibiskupství palác)

Hradčanské náměstí, 16, Hradčany. Tram 22: Pražský hrad. Interior open to the public only the day before Good Friday.

Built in the Italian Renaissance style, this stately residence has been the seat of the Archdiocese of Prague since 1562; it hosted Pope John Paul II during his visit to the city in 1990. The palace, one of many architectural sites on Castle Square, underwent several reconstructions, first in 1669–1674 by Jean-Baptiste Mathey in the early Baroque style and then in 1764–1765, by Johann Birch, who is responsible for the building's current Rococo look. The interior rooms, open to the public one day each year, feature exquisite tapestries and ecclesiastical paintings.

Wallenstein Palace

Hvězda Summer Palace
(Letohrádek Hvězda)

Na Vypichu, Liboc. Tram 18: Petříny. Open May–Sept Tue–Sun 10am–6pm, Apr & Oct Tue–Sun 10am–5pm. 30 Kč. 220 516 695.

In the quiet suburb of Liboc, the Hvězda Summer Palace is a unique example of Renaissance architecture. The two-story villa is built in the shape of a six-pointed star, from which it derives its name (hvězda means "star" in Czech), and it is covered with bossage. Constructed at the behest of Archduke Ferdinand of Tirol between 1555 and 1558, Hvězda now houses an exhibit about the 1620 **Battle of Bíla Hora**, which took place nearby.

Kinský Palace
(Palác Kinských)

*Staroměstské náměstí 12, **Old Town**. Metro A: Staroměstská. Open year-round Tue–Sun 10am–6pm. Closed Mon. 224 810 758.*

Kinský Palace exterior is Prague's finest example of Rococo architecture, although the building's interior is Baroque in style. Its prominent position on Old Town Square makes it impossible to miss. Built over ten years (1755–1765), the palace now hosts an outlet of the **National Gallery** *(see Museums)*. Kinský Palace also once housed a grammar school, attended by **Franz Kafka** from 1893 to 1901.

Silva-Taroucca Palace
(Palác Sylva-Taroucca)

Na Příkopě 10, New Town. Metro A or B: Můstek.

One of many interesting sites on the busy shopping street **Na Příkopě** *(see Shopping)*, this structure dates to 1751, a magnificent structure in the Rococo style that was the shared project of architects **Kilián Ignác Dientzenhofer** and **Anselmo Lurago**. Today it houses office and retail space. The statues on the cornices that reinforce the palace are the work of Ignác Platzer the Elder.

Tuscany Palace
(Toskánský palace)

Hradčanské náměstí 5, Hradčany. Tram 22: Pražský hrad.

This exemplary Baroque building, which currently houses the Ministry of Foreign Affairs, was erected between 1689 and 1691 and designed by architect Jean-Baptiste Mathey. The five statues poised on the roof were sculpted by Ferdinand Maximilian Brokoff.

Žofín Palace
(Palác Žofín)

Slovanský ostrov 226, New Town. Trams 2, 6, 9 or 18: Národní divadlo.

Slavonic Island, on which this palace sits, didn't exist until the 18C, when the river sediments settled. Built in the 1840s, Žofín Palace opened to host choral concerts in its grand ballrooms, and in the 1930s, **Žofín Garden** restaurant *(see Must Eat)* was added. Since suffering damage in the 2002 floods, both Žofín and Slavonic Island have been extensively restored.

PALACES

ARCHITECTURAL LANDMARKS

Prague is famous the world over for its architecture, and wandering the cobbled streets admiring the façades is something everyone can appreciate. The city illustrates a chronology of architectural styles, dating from the Romanesque through the Gothic to the bold Rondo-Cubist and the harsh Socialist Functionalist styles of the 20C. Prague's buildings tell its story in brick and stone, a tale of enlightenment, oppression and subsequent artistic freedom.

Astronomical Clock★★★
(Orloj)

Old Town Hall, Staroměstské náměstí 1/3, Old Town. Metro A: Staroměstská.

Appealing to all ages, the 1410 Astronomical Clock is a true medieval wonder. Three hands of the central face indicate, along with the passing of the hours, the position of the sun, moon and planets according to medieval cosmology. The lower face is a marvelous calendar of the months of the year. Be sure to show up

on the hour between 9am and 9pm, when the clock stages a mechanical procession of the twelve apostles accompanied by trumpeting sculpted skeletons. Originally installed by royal clockmaker **Mikulas of Kadane**, in cooperation with Jan Sindel, mathematics and astronomy professor at Charles University, the Astronomical Clock was improved by Master Hanuš around 1490, and perfected by Jan Táborský in the mid-16C.

Charles Bridge★★★
(Karlův most)

Spans Old Town to Lesser Town; from Old Town, Metro A: Staroměstská.

Charles Bridge is Prague's most instantly recognizable landmark. Completed in the early 15C, the span has shaped the history of Prague. Connecting what is now the Old Town and the Lesser Town, the bridge replaced an earlier one, known as the Judith Bridge, and strengthened Prague's role as a trade route between the East and West. Architect Petr Parléř, who also designed **St. Vitus Cathedral★★★** *(see Religious Sites)*, was responsible for the Gothic-style Bohemian sandstone bridge. On the Old Town

Astronomical Clock

©Prague Information Service

Lucky St. John

The most famous statue on **Charles Bridge★★★** is that of **St. John of Nepomuk** (1345–1393), which is usually surrounded by tourists trying to rub his foot for good luck. An earlier legend, however, says to seek out the small brass cross on the bridge's wall about halfway across, marking the spot where St. John was believed to have been cast over the side for defending the Catholic Church. Place your left hand over the cross, and place your right foot on the small brass button on the ground; legend has it if you make a wish from here, your wish will be granted within a year and a day.

side, the bridge is topped by the **Old Town Bridge Tower★★** *(see Historic Sites)*, and on the other side, by the **Lesser Town Bridge Tower** *(see Historic Sites)*. Commissioned by King Charles IV, the bridge was rumored to have incorporated egg yolks into its construction – this being the reason it has withstood centuries of floods. Several years ago, scientists confirmed that egg proteins were indeed used in the ancient mortar. The cobblestone-lined bridge was open to vehicular traffic until 1965; today, the traffic is all pedestrian. The 30 **statues★★** along the 516m/1,693ft-long span are all replicas; the originals are on view at the National Museum's **Lapidarium**, at the Výstaviště Exhibition Grounds, in Holešovice.

Municipal House★★★
(Obecní dům)

Náměstí Republiky 5, Old Town. Metro B: Náměstí Republiky. Open year-round daily 10am–7pm. Free entry to the front hall and basement; other rooms accessible by guided tour only, 280 Kč. 222 002 101. www.obecni-dum.cz.

Built to be a true representation of Czech architectural accomplishment, this palace is one of Prague's most notable Art Nouveau landmarks. It was designed by

Antonín Balšánek and **Osvald Polívka** between 1906 and 1911. The central dome epitomizes the Secessionist style.

Inside, **Smetana Hall★★** – which now hosts cultural events – is embellished with statues and paintings, and is lit from above by a round stained-glass window. Don't miss the **ceremonial rooms★★** on the second floor, adorned with mirrors, pale woodwork and delicate stucco decoration. Municipal House also contains Francouzská *(see Must Eat)* and a charming café *(see side-bar, p 64).*

Dancing House★★
(Tančící dům)

Rašínovo nábřeží 80, New Town. Trams 14 or 17: Jiráskovo náměstí. Closed to the public except the rooftop restaurant.

Creating a storm of controversy when it was unveiled in 1996, this postmodern office building was designed by the renowned Canadian-born architect **Frank Gehry**. The towers seem to sway gleefully, earning them the nickname "Ginger and Fred" after the famous dancing couple who starred in many American musicals in the 1930s.

ARCHITECTURAL LANDMARKS

63

Golden Lane

©Prague Information Service

Secessionist Buildings★★

Národní třída 7 and 9, north side, New Town. Metro B: Narodni třída.

A Czech version of the Art Nouveau style that flourished in Europe at the turn of the 20C, the Secession movement used glass, ceramics, ironwork and floral motifs. These two office buildings on National Avenue, built by **Osvald Polívka** between 1903 and 1908, are among the most elegant Secessionist buildings in the city – despite being in need of a facelift. Their façades combine precise lines with rich, but not excessive, adornments.

Café Obecni dům

www.vysehrad2000.cz.
Considered one of Prague's most beautiful cafés, the Secession-era eatery on the ground floor of the **Municipal House★★★** *(see p63)* is the place to go for coffee and cake – a specialty from the on-site confectionary – in an opulent setting. Inside, grandeur abounds in the sculpted Art Nouveau walls, gilded mirrors and crystal chandeliers, where you can sit and contemplate empires . . . or just lunch.

Golden Lane★
(Zlatá ulička)

Within Prague Castle complex, Hradčany. Tram 22: Pražský hrad. Open daily Apr–Oct 9am–6pm, Jan–Mar 9am–4pm. Entry combined with long (350 Kč) or short (250 Kč) Prague Castle tour. 224 373 368. www.hrad.cz.

Walking down Golden Lane, named for the legendary medieval alchemists said to have lived here during the reign of Rudolf II, is a trip back in time. The line of tiny houses, built directly into the castle walls in the late 16C, was created for the marksmen of the castle guard. Today, the buildings house souvenir shops and the cobblestones echo with tourists' footsteps.

House of the Black Madonna★
(Dům U černe Matky boži)

Celetná 34, Old Town. Metro B: Náměstí Republiky. Entry only for museum and café.

This house gets its name from the statue of the Virgin Mary that adorns one of its façades; this is all that remains of the original Baroque house. Built in 1911, the current Rondo-Cubist building is a shining example of the work of architect **Josef Gočár**. Today it holds a café, a bookstore specializing in photography, and the **Czech Museum of Cubism** (see Museums).

Prague City Savings Bank★
(Živnostenská banka)

Na Příkopě 20, New Town. Metro A or B: Můstek. 224 121 111.

A magnificent 1896 Renaissance Revival building designed by Osvald Polívka was built to house the seat of the provincial bank. On a level with the great national monuments of the city center, the bank is lavishly decorated on every side by great artists: Mikoláš Aleš, Stanislav Sucharda, Max Švabinský, and Bohuslav Schnirch. Inside the heavy gold doors, the principal attraction is its **main hall**, on the second floor. From its mosaic floor to its stained-glass ceiling, the bank's ornate decoration certainly would have convinced any prospective investor of the Bohemian kingdom's potential.

Hotel Jalta

Václavské náměstí 45, New Town. Metro A or C: Muzeum.

On Wenceslas Square, this lodging is one of the city's standout representations of the Socialist Realism style mandated by the Soviets and based on the Stalin-era constructions in the Soviet Union. Opened in 1958, Hotel Jalta was designed by the young architect Antonín Tenzer. Note the statues of a farmer and his wife on the hotel's terrace; romanticizing the common worker was typical of the era.

New World★★

Follow the sign off Castle Square. You've likely heard of **Golden Lane★**, and so has everyone else, as the crowds there can attest. But just a few steps away is **Nový svět** (New World). These few cobblestone lanes lined with pastel-painted medieval houses exhibit all the Old World charm of its golden neighbor.

Storch House
(Štorchův dům)

Staroměstské náměstí 16, Old Town. Metro A: Staroměstská. Closed to the public.

While there are many marvels on **Old Town Square★★★**, this house, at No. 16, is an architectural gem and a protected monument of Prague. It was built between 1867 and 1868 by architect Friedrich Ohmann and decorated in the Vladislav Gothic style by artist Mikoláš Aleš. The paintings on the façade depict St. Wenceslas.

Žižkov TV Tower

Mahlerovy sady 1, Žižkov. Metro A: Jiřího z Poděbrad. Observation deck open daily 10am–10pm. 120 Kč. 724 251 286. www.praguerocket.cz.

The highest point on the Prague skyline, the modern television tower (1992) rises more than 200m/656ft, thus earning its nickname, "the rocket." In 2000, artist David Černy installed the crawling babies on the tower. Take the elevator up to the **observation deck** for an amazing view.

RELIGIOUS SITES

It's practically impossible to walk a block in Prague without coming across an imposing church or synagogue. The Czech Republic may be the world's most atheistic country, but its past is steeped in religion. From Prague's days as the seat of the Holy Roman Empire to the devastation of the city's Jewish quarter, the city's religious sites serve as timeless monuments to the people who have worshipped within their walls and the stories that unfolded just beyond their doors.

Church of St. Nicholas★★★
(Sv. Mikuláše)

Malostranské náměstí, Lesser Town. Tram 20 or 22: Malostranské náměstí. Church open Mar–Oct daily 9am–5pm, Nov–Feb 9am–4pm. Tower open daily Apr–Sep 10am–10pm, Oct & Mar 9am–8pm, Nov–Feb 10am–6pm. 100 Kč.

Not to be confused with the church of the same name on Old Town Square *(see p70)* – although they were completed by the same architect, **Kilián Ignác Dientzenhofer**, in the Baroque style – this St. Nicholas Church dates to 1703. Its copper dome and bell tower are a recognizable part of the Lesser Town skyline, and the church's organ – still in use for the frequent concerts held here – was once played by Mozart in 1787 during his residence in Prague. Inside the dome, note the fresco depicting the *Celebration of the Holy Trinity* by Franz Palko.

Loreto Prague★★★
(Loreta)

Loretánské náměstí 7, Hradčany. Tram 22: Pražský hrad. Open Apr–Oct daily 9am–12:15pm & 1pm–5pm; Nov–Mar 9:30am–12:15pm & 1pm–4pm. 110 Kč. 220 516 740. www.loreta.cz.

A Baroque pilgrimage site, the Loreto Prague was designed as a self-contained complex of buildings centering on the **Santa Casa★**, or Holy House *(see sidebar, opposite)*. Originally a simple structure, the Santa Casa was decorated as early as 1664 with bas-reliefs depicting the life of Mary. The stucco and bricks, less noble materials than those used to decorate the church, represent the modest conditions in which the the Holy Family lived.
Giovanni Battista Orsi built **Our Lady of Loreta** church between 1626 and 1631. In the18C, Kilián Ignác Dientzenhofer raised the courtyard a level and designed

The Watchtower

Recently opened to the public, the tower of the **Church of St. Nicholas★★★** once served a more sinister purpose. Under the Communist regime that ended in 1989, the secret police used the tower to keep an eye on the quarter's citizens. Once you see the view from here over the rooftops of the Lesser Town, it's easy to understand why. Today, the tower contains a small exhibit about the secret police *(open daily Apr–Sept 10am–10pm, Oct & Mar 9am–8pm, Nov–Feb 10am–6pm; 100 Kč).*

MUST SEE

Loreta Prague

©Egmont Strigl/age fotostock

the **west façade★★** with its monumental statues. Overlooking the courtyard, the clock tower contains a 17C **carillon** that plays a melody composed by Dvořák. In the north and south wings of the cloister, you'll see richly decorated chapels; in the center of the courtyard stands a large statue representing *The Resurrection*. Originally a much smaller building, the **Church of the Nativity of Our Lord★★★** boasts one of the most ornate Baroque interiors in Prague, especially rich with frescoes, statuary and oratories. The **Treasury★★** contains chalices, monstrances (used to display the consecrated Eucharist during Mass) and a host of religious objects spanning the 16C–18C. The most extraordinary monstrance, the 1699 **Prague Sun★★**, is set with 6,500 diamonds.

Old-New Synagogue★★★
(Staronová synagoga)

Maiselova 18, Josefov. Metro A: Staroměstská. Open Nov–March 9:30am–5pm, Apr–Oct 9:30am–6pm, daily except for Saturdays and Jewish holidays. 200 Kč. 224 800 812. www.synagogue.cz.

Holy House

The original Holy House (or Santa Casa) stood in Nazareth in Palestine, and was said to be the site where the archangel Gabriel announced to the Virgin Mary that she would conceive a child of the Holy Spirit – a virgin birth. This is also where the Holy Family lived after their return from exile in Egypt. In the 13C, pilgrims dismantled the house and transported it in sections to Loreto, Italy.

The most picturesque of the ghetto buildings, the Old-New Synagogue is the oldest operational synagogue in Europe, dating back to 1270. And as one of the three remaining synagogues in Prague (along with the High Synagogue and the Jerusalem Synagogue) that still hold regular services, it forms the heart of Prague's Jewish community. As you enter, look up at the tympanum that crowns the entrance. The twelve roots of the vine sculpted in bas-relief represent the twelve tribes of Israel, and the four vine stocks represent the four rivers of creation. In the center of the double nave, surrounded by a

RELIGIOUS SITES

The Golem

The legend of the Golem plays a special role in Prague mythology. The Golem, a mythical character in Jewish folklore, is an anthropomorphic being made of clay who was supposedly brought to life in the 16C by rabbi Judah Loew ben Bezalel to protect the Jews in Prague's ghetto. A fictionalized account of the story was told in the 1914 novel *The Golem* by Gustav Meyrink. The Golem's remains are said to be contained in the attic of the **Old-New Synagogue★★★** *(see p67)*.

Gothic rail, you'll see the *bimah* or *almemar*, a platform from which the Torah scrolls are read. Near the eastern wall is the ark containing the Torah. Windows allow women to follow the service from an adjacent room.

St. Vitus Cathedral★★★
(Chrám Sv. Víta)

Within Prague Castle complex, Hradčany (enter between the second and third courtyards). Tram 22: Pražský hrad. Open Mar–Oct Mon–Sat 9am–6pm, Sun noon–6pm; Nov–Feb Mon–Sat 9am–4pm, Sun noon–4pm. Admission included with Prague Castle tour, 250 Kč. 224 373 368. www.hrad.cz.

From the skyline, visitors often mistake the iconic spires of St. Vitus Cathedral for **Prague Castle★★★**, the surrounding complex of buildings. But the soaring structure– a symbol of the Czech state – with its flourish of flying buttresses is actually located inside the castle grounds. Surprisingly, St. Vitus is not as old as it looks; while construction of a Gothic cathedral began here in 1344 at the behest of King Charles IV, the structure did not gain its grand neo-Gothic façade until the early 20C; it was consecrated in 1929 for the thousand-year anniversary of St. Wenceslas – the

country's patron saint.

Walk around to the south side of the cathedral, where a **Venetian mosaic★★** on the **Golden Gate** depicts the *Last Judgement*. Upon entering the church, your eye will be drawn to the dazzling **stained glass★★**. In 1928 František Kysela used 25,000 pieces of glass to create the rose window on the western wall. Equally amazing is the **Baroque vault★★** of St. John of Nepomuk, made in 1736 from nearly two tons of pure silver. Brave the crowds waiting to see the **Chapel of St. Wenceslas★★**, whose gilded walls are covered with semiprecious stones. Then tackle the breathtaking ascent to the top of the **Bell Tower**, a total of 287 steps, and you'll be rewarded with an unimpeded **view★★** over the castle complex and gardens, and beyond.

Basilica of St. George★★
(Bazilika Sv. Jiří)

Jiřské náměstí, Hradčany. Tram 22: Pražský hrad. Open Apr–Oct 9am–6pm, Nov–Mar 9am–4pm. Closed Dec. 24. Admission included with Prague Castle tour, 250 Kč. 224 373 368. www.hrad.cz.

The loveliest Roman edifice still standing in the country, this basilica in the Prague Castle complex was consecrated in 925,

MUST SEE

when the relics of **St. Ludmila** – grandmother of St. Wenceslas and one of the patron saints of Bohemia – were deposited here. The original building was destroyed in the 12C and reconstructed later. Its Baroque façade, added between 1657 and 1680, contrasts notably with the basilica's two Roman towers. The pediment on the façade shows St. George struggling with a dragon.

Church of Our Lady Before Týn★★
(Matky Boží před Týnem)

Old Town Square, Old Town (enter through the gate of Staroměstské náměstí 14). Metro A: Staroměstská. Open Tue–Sat 10:30am–1pm & 3pm–5pm, Sun 10:30am–noon. Closed Mon. 20 Kč donation. 222 318 160.

This church's two spires, rising to 80m/262ft high and visible from a large part of the city, have become one of the symbols of Prague, despite the façade not being fully

Tycho Brahe

Mystery surrounds Tycho Brahe, who is entombed in the **Church of Our Lady Before Týn★★**. The death of the Danish astronomer in 1601 has long been the subject of debate, as contention has held that he was poisoned by his colleague, Johannes Kepler. Brahe, a key figure in the court of Rudolf II, was exhumed in November 2010 in a bid to put to rest the rumors of his murder. While no conclusive evidence of murder was found, the exhumation did reveal the body of a mysterious woman (who was not his wife) buried next to him.

visible from Old Town Square. This is the largest religious edifice on this side of the Vltava River, built between 1365 and 1470 in a radiant Gothic style. The interior is decorated in a rich mix of Gothic, Baroque and Renaissance styles, and includes the tomb of the Danish astronomer Tycho Brahe *(see sidebar, above)*.

Church of Our Lady Before Týn

©Prague Information Service

RELIGIOUS SITES

69

Church of St. Francis Seraphicus★★
(Sv. Františka)

Křižovnické náměstí, Old Town. Metro A: Staroměstská. Open for services only, and for concerts Apr–Nov.

A masterpiece of religious Baroque architecture, at the Old Town entrance to Charles Bridge, this church was built between 1679 and 1689 by Jean-Baptiste Mathey, assisted by Italian architect Carlo Lurago. It is owned by the only Order of Knights in the Czech Republic, the Order of Knights of the Cross with a Red Star. Inside are interesting displays and occasional organ concerts.

Church of St. John on the Rock★★
(Sv. Jana Nepomuckého na Skalce)

Vyšehrdaská 49, New Town. Tram 18 or 24: Botanická zahrada. Open only for services.

Church of St. Nicholas

Built as early as 1730, this marvel of geometric complexity is the work of the Baroque architect **Kilián Ignác Dientzenhofer**. While you'll appreciate the harmonious outside contours of the façade, you'll also have to stop there, as the interior is only open for church services. The windows of the church, arranged at differing levels, help give the building its dynamic effect.

Church of St. Nicholas★★
(Sv. Mikuláše)

Corner of Old Town Square at Pařížská, Old Town. Metro A: Staroměstská. Open Mon noon–4pm, Tue–Sat 10am–4pm.

Since the destruction of the north side of the Old Town Hall, the façade of St. Nicholas is visible from the square. This splendid Baroque building (1732–37) was designed by Prague-based architect Kilián Ignác Dientzenhofer. While the exterior – featuring twin towers and a central dome – resembles many churches in Prague, the interior is much more elaborate, especially the stucco decorations by Bernard Spinetti. The frescoes that cover the inside of the cupola represent the life of St. Nicholas. During the tourist season, concerts are held here almost daily.

Pinkas Synagogue★★
(Pinkasova synagoga)

Široká 23/3, Josefov. Metro A: Staroměstská. Open Apr–Oct 9am–6pm; Nov–Mar 9am–4:30pm. Closed Sat & Jewish holidays. 300 Kč (combination ticket; see Touring Tip). 222 317 191. www.jewishmuseum.cz.

Patricia Grube/Michelin

Built in 1535, Pinkas Synagogue is the second oldest of the Jewish Town. Inside, a vaulted nave of Gothic style borders a lateral nave of Renaissance style, added to the original building between 1607 and 1625 to accommodate women separately. After serving centuries as a private synagogue, the building is today open to the public and dedicated to the 77,297 Jews of Bohemia and Moravia who perished in the Holocaust; the names of all the victims are written on the wall. The Communists whitewashed the wall in the 1950s, but the inscriptions were painstakingly restored in the early 1990s.

Strahov Monastery★★
(Strahovský klášter)

Strahovské nádvoří 1, Hradčany. Tram 22: Pohořelec. Open Tue–Sun 9am–12pm, 12:30pm–5pm. 80 Kč. 233 107 711. www.strahov monastery.cz.

Founded in 1140, Strahov Monastery was designed in the purest Roman style. Its current Baroque appearance mainly dates back to the 17C and 18C. Entering the courtyard by the main

Touring Tip

If you purchase a ticket to visit the **Pinkas Synagogue★★**, that same ticket will grant you admission to the **Old Jewish Cemetery★★★** *(see Historic Sites)* and all the synagogues in Josefov that are open to the public, except the **Old-New Synagogue★★★**.

entrance, you will first notice the **Church of St. Roch** (Sv. Rocha), built between 1603 and 1611 in a characteristic Bohemian Gothic style. Nearby is the **Basilica of the Assumption of Our Lady★★★** (Nanebevzetí panny Marie), which still exhibits its 1143 Roman design, despite many later renovations. Here lie the remains of **St. Norbert**, founder of the Premonstratensian order to which the monastery belongs. The life of the saint is depicted in the decorative frescoes in the church. The monastery also houses an **art gallery**, the largest in Bohemia, featuring 1,000 works from the Czech Gothic movement as well as paintings by 17C and 18C Flemish and Italian masters.

Strahov Library★★★

Don't leave the **Strahov Monastery★★** without a visit to the Strahov Library (Strahovská Knihovna), among the most beautiful libraries in the world. The incredible ornamented rooms contain more than 200,000 old manuscripts, dating back to the 16C, as well as rare prints. Not all of the rooms are accessible, but they can be viewed from their roped entrances. **Theological Hall★★★** is the oldest in the library, built between 1671 and1679 according to the design of Giovanni Domenico Orsini. Note the huge vaulted ceiling and the stuccoes interspersed with early 18C paintings. **Philosophical Hall★★★** follows a more classic linear design. On the ceiling, a superb fresco by Franz Anton Maulpertsch tells the story of humanity and philosophy.

RELIGIOUS SITES

Church of Our Lady Beneath the Chain★
(Panny Marie pod řetězem)

*Lázeňská, **Lesser Town**. Tram 20 or 22: Hellichova. Open only for services.*

The large Roman basilica built by the Knights of the Maltese Cross close to Charles Bridge was almost entirely demolished in the 14C to make way for the Gothic sanctuary of Our Lady Beneath the Chain. But the Hussite Wars took precedence, and the church was never finished. Today, the bases of the twin towers with their buttresses and massive masonry remain. St. John of Nepomuk was arrested here in 1393 before being thrown into the Vltava River.

Church of St. Ignatius★
(Sv. Ignáce)

*Ječná 2, **New Town**. Metro B: Karlovo náměstí. 221 990 200. Open only for services.*

Along with the neighboring school, which occupies half of the square, this church constitutes the seat of the Jesuit Order in the New Town. Built between 1665 and 1670 by Italian architect Carlo Lurago, the church is the third-largest Jesuit complex in Europe. It gives praise to the founder of the order, St. Ignatius of Loyola, whose statue perches on the gable.

Church of St. James★
(Sv. Jakuba)

*Malá Štupartská 6, **Old Town**. Metro B: Náměstí Republiky. Open Mon–Sat 9:30am–12:15pm, 2–4pm; Sun except services.*

Tucked away at a crossroads of cobbled streets, the second-largest church in Prague is renowned for its incredible acoustics, as well as its 1702 organ, still used for concerts here. St. James houses 23 chapels, and its vast length recalls its Gothic origins. Finished at the end of the 14C, the internal structure remains under magnificent layers of Baroque ornamentation. The façade shows off three late 17C bas-relief stuccoes by Ottavio Mosto. In the north wing, the **Jan Václav Vratislav of Mitrovice monument**★ was designed by Fischer von Erlach.

When you leave, don't be startled by the dried hand hanging to the right of the entrance. Legend says it is the hand of a thief who tried to steal a wooden statue of the Virgin Mary. In the process, she grabbed his hand so firmly that it was impossible to free him. The only solution was to cut his hand off. Exhibited here, the severed hand serves as a warning to other would-be wrongdoers.

Church of St James

Church of St. Thomas

©Artur Bogacki/iStockphoto

Church of St. Salvator★
(Sv. Salvátora)

Karlova and Křížovnické náměstí, Old Town. Metro A: Staroměstská. Visitor access through the Clementinum (see Historic Sites).

This church is part of the architectural ensemble of the **Clementinum**★★ complex, which comprises three churches in all. The construction on St. Salvator began in 1578 in a Renaissance style, but its renovation in 1640 by the architect Carlo Lurago gave the church its current Baroque air. The statues of the façade are the work of the sculptor Jan Bendl.

Church of St. Thomas★
(Sv. Tomáše)

Josefská 8, Lesser Town. Tram 12, 20 or 22: Malostranské náměstí. Open Mon–Sat 11am–1pm & 2pm–5pm, Sun 9am–noon & 430–5:30pm. 221 714 444.

One of Prague's oldest churches, St. Thomas was built in the 1300s and belonged to the Augustinians. In later years the church underwent several transformations, including one in the 18C by Kilián Ignác Dientzenhofer, who reworked it in the Baroque style. The interior

is exceptionally opulent, owing to the contribution of painters such as Karel Škréta, who accomplished the tableau of the Holy Trinity, and Peter-Paul Rubens, who decorated the high altar.

Church of St. Ursula★
(Sv. Voršily)

Národní třída 8, New Town. Metro B: Národní třída. Open only for services.

Built between 1698 and 1704 by Marco Antonio Canevale for the convent of the Ursulines, this is one of the first churches to exhibit the late Baroque style in Prague. If the church appears from the street like it's built on its side, that's because it is; Canevale had to design the church to fit between the existing houses. The magnificently restored interior touts statues by Ferdinand Preiss, an altar painting of St. Ursula by K. Liška, and an illustration of the Assumption by Petr Brandl.

Church of Sts. Peter and Paul★

V pevnosti 5b, Vyšehrad. Metro C: Vyšehrad. Open Mon–Sun 9am–noon & 1pm–5pm. Closed Tue. 10 Kc. 249 113 53.

This neo-Gothic church, framed by the medieval **Fortress of Vyšehrad**★ *(see Historic Sites)*, is rivaled in scale only by **St. Vitus Cathedral**★★★, which it resembles in appearance. Set dramatically on a rocky hill along the Vltava, the church was built by King Vratislav II in the 11C. It was rebuilt in the 14C as a high Gothic church before gaining its current appearance in the late 19C.

Church of Sts. Peter and Paul

©Artur Bogacki/iStockphoto

Emmaus Convent★
(Emauzy klášter na Slovanech)

Vyšehradská 49. New Town. Tram 18 or 24: Botanická zahrada. 221 979 211. Open Mon–Fri 8am–6pm. 30 Kč.

This religious institution founded by Charles IV and run by Croatian Benedictines was established to bring the Oriental and Occidental churches closer together. The bell tower, part of which was accidentally destroyed by an Allied bomb in World War II, was replaced by a double spire during the Communist regime. The **cloister** contains beautiful frescoes.

Italian Chapel★
(Vlašská kaple)

Karlova, Old Town. Metro A: Staroměstská. Open only for services.

Part of the **Clementinum**★★ complex *(see Historic Sites)*, this ravishing little Renaissance-style chapel, built around 1600, was one of the first buildings with a central layout of this type north of the Alps. Fashioned to serve the considerable Italian community in Prague at the time, the chapel's perfect oval design was considered revolutionary.

Our Lady of the Snows Basilica★
(Panny Marie Sněžné)

Jungmannovo náměstí 18, New Town. Metro A or B: Můstek. 222 246 243. Open only for services.

In 1347, Emperor Charles IV undertook the project of having this church built, but only lived to see the choir completed. Its vaulting is the highest in Prague at 34m/111.5ft. The large Gothic building easily accommodated the Baroque additions on the interior. An especially nice view of the church, largely hidden from view at other angles, can be seen from the nearby **Franciscan Gardens**★ *(see Parks and Gardens)*.

Church of Our Lady of Victory – Infant Jesus of Prague
(Panny Marie Vítezná - Pražské Jezulátko)

Karmelitská 9. Lesser Town. Tram 12, 20 or 22: Malostranské náměstí. Open daily 8:30am–6pm

MUST SEE

Emmaus Convent

©Mary C Legg/age fotostock

(Sat & Sun 8pm). 257 533 646. www.pragjesu.info.

Completed in 1640 for the Lutherans as the Church of the Saint Trinity, this edifice bears the Baroque style. After the Battle of White Mountain in 1620, the church, then in the hands of the Carmelites, was renamed for the Habsburgs' victory. Our Lady of Victory contains the **Infant Jesus of Prague**, a wax figurine set with precious stones given to the Carmelites in 1628 by the Princess of Lobkowicz. According to legend, this figurine has carried out numerous miracles, including protecting the city from the great plague that spread through Europe after the Seven Years' War (1756-63). Thousands of people come to the church to pay homage to the Infant of Prague each year.

Maisel Synagogue
(Maiselova synagoga)

Maiselova 8–10, Josefov. Metro A: Staroměstská. Open Apr–Oct 9am–6pm; Nov–Mar: 9am–4:30pm. Closed Sat & Jewish holidays. 300 Kč (ticket valid for the Old Jewish Cemetery and all the synagogues except the Old-New Synagogue). 222 317 191. www.jewishmuseum.cz.

Built in 1592, the Maisel Synagogue was twice damaged by fire, and was finally rebuilt in 1905 in the Gothic Revival style. It houses a superb collection of silver objects and an exhibit on the development of the Jewish community up to its emancipation in the 18C, a display that continues in the opulent 1868 **Spanish Synagogue** nearby *(Vězeňská 1, Josefov; same hours and website as Maisel; 224 819 464).*

Rotunda of the Holy Cross
(Rotunda Sv. Kříže)

Corner of Konviktska and Karoliny Světlé, Old Town. Metro B: Národní třída. Open only for services.

As a rare example of Roman architecture (from the second half of the 11C), this rotunda stands out among the more "modern" buildings of the Old Town. The rotunda takes its name from the legend of a young girl who was crucified for her Christian beliefs and thrown into a lake that once stood on this site. It is said that her cross reared up later during a storm, as a sign from God.

75

MONUMENTS AND MEMORIALS

Sometimes it seems every public square, garden or even street corner in Prague has a monument to someone. In the capital, statues and memorials are plentiful and varied, from centuries-old reminders of martyrdom and sainthood to the artistic endeavors of the more recent past.

Jan Hus Memorial★★
(Pomnik Jana Husa)

Staroměstské náměstí, Old Town. Metro A: Staroměstská.

Focal point of **Old Town Square**★★★ *(see Historic Squares)*, this awe-inspiring statue depicts the martyred Hussite leader **Jan Hus** (1369–1415), whose opposition to certain doctrines of the Catholic Church paved the way for the Protestant movement in the 16C. Hus was burned at the stake in 1415. The statue was unveiled in 1915, the 500th anniversary of his death.

Statue of St. Wenceslas★★

Top of Wenceslas Square (in front of the National Museum), New Town. Metro A or C: Muzeum.

As befitting his namesake square, the country's patron saint is immortalized at the top of **Wenceslas Square**★★★

(see Historic Squares). Here his equestrian statue, a popular meeting point, presides over the boulevard and oversees the daily goings-on of Prague. Though it was designed in 1887 by **Josef Vaclav Myslbek**, the statue was not completed until 1924.

Franz Kafka Monument★

Intersection of Dušní and Vězeňská Sts., Josefov. Metro A: Staroměstská.

This 3.75m/12ft-high bronze statue was erected in 2003 for the 120th anniversary of the birth of writer **Franz Kafka** (1883–1924). Sculptor Jaroslav Róna took his inspiration from one of the author's short stories, "Description of a Struggle," which recounts a man's stroll through Prague perched on another man's shoulders. He thus shows Kafka perched on the shoulders of a giant with no head and no arms.

Preserved in Death

The suicide of young **Jan Palach** initiated widespread protests against the Communist regime, with thousands filling the streets of Prague for an impromptu funeral march when Palach died in January 1969. Olbram Zoubek, a sculptor and fellow student, secretly made a death mask of Palach, which was cast in bronze. After the Velvet Revolution of 1989, the mask was mounted on the wall of Charles University's Arts Faculty building in what is now **Jan Palach Square**.

Statue of Charles IV★

*Křižovnické náměstí, **Old Town**. Metro A: Staroměstská.*

Before crossing Charles Bridge from Old Town, take a moment to doff your hat at the statue of Emperor Charles IV on **Crusaders' Square★★** *(see Historic Squares)*. Known as the "father of the Czech nation," Charles IV reigned from 1347 until his death in 1378, and was also crowned Holy Roman Emperor in 1355. His statue was placed in the square in 1848 in celebration of the 500th anniversary of Charles University, which is named for the monarch.

Jan Palach Memorial

*Immediately in front of National Museum on Wenceslas Square, **New Town**. Metro A or C: Muzeum.*

This memorial is easy to miss. Make sure to look down at the cobblestones for the raised bronze cross, which commemorates the spot where Charles University student **Jan Palach** (born 1948) committed suicide by setting himself on fire on January 16, 1969, in protest of the Soviet occupation.

The Metronome

*Letná Park, above intersection of Svatopluk Čech Bridge and nábř. Edvarda Beneše St., **Letná**. Tram 12 or 17: Čechův most.*

Overlooking Prague, on the granite pedestal that was once the plinth of a giant monument to Stalin, stands a massive kinetic sculpture by Czech artist Vratislav Novak. His 23m/75ft-tall functional metronome was erected in 1991.

Monument to the Victims of Communism

*Bottom of Petřín Hill, **Lesser Town**. Tram 6, 9, 12, 20 or 22: Újezd.*

A harsh but powerful aesthetic pervades this work by Olbram Zoubek. Installed in 2002, it depicts a series of bronze figures in states of gradual disappearance. The monument is set at intervals in descending stairs, representing the torment of political prisoners under the Communist regime.

Monument to the Victims of Communism

©Prague Information Service

National Memorial at Vítkov
(Národní památník na Vítkově)

*U Památníku 1900, **Žižkov**. Trams 5, 9 or 26: Lipanská. www.nm.cz.*

One of the world's largest equestrian statues tops Vitkov Hill. At 9m/30ft high, the bronze of Czech general **Jan Žižka** (1360–1424) weighs 16.5 tons. The massive structure behind it is the **National Monument** *(open Tue–Sun 10am–6pm; 110 Kc; 222 781 676)*, built in 1938 to honor the Czech soldiers who fought in WWII.

HISTORIC SITES

Prague has long served as a crossroads for historical events, its location in the heart of Europe giving it inimitable significance in both ancient trade routes and contemporary European affairs. The Golden City even had a stint as the seat of the Holy Roman Empire under Emperor and King Charles IV. Today, the very air of Prague is steeped in history, and nearly every building and street has a story to tell – if you stop to listen.

Old Jewish Cemetery★★★
(Starý židovský hřbitov)

Široká 3, Josefov. Metro A: Staroměstská. Open Apr–Oct 9am–6 pm, Nov–Mar 9am– 4:30pm. Closed Sat & Jewish holidays. 300 Kč (ticket includes all the synagogues except the Old–New Synagogue; see Religious Sites). 224 819 464. www.jewishmuseum.cz.

One of the oldest Jewish cemeteries in Europe, laid out in the early 15C, this plot creates a striking visual effect with its myriad vertical headstones. The oldest known tomb here, that of the rabbi-poet Avigdor Kara, dates back to 1439. In the space of three and a half centuries, 100,000 Jewish people were buried here, although the cemetery has only 12,000 graves. The oldest ones are simple sandstone slabs bearing Hebrew inscriptions.

From the 16C onward, the graves were decorated with sculptures and bas-reliefs symbolizing the trade of the deceased; the numerous animals in relief represent the name of the person buried there. Engraved with the history of the deceased, marble slabs showed up in the 17C.
Also on the cemetery grounds are two sites that are part of the

Touring Tip

Men are required to cover their heads upon entering the **Old Jewish Cemetery★★★**. Any hats are acceptable, but if you don't have one, paper hats are provided onsite.

Jewish Museum: the **Klausen Synagogue** (U starého hřbitova), which contains a collection of objects illustrating Jewish traditions and customs; and the **Ceremonial Hall** (Obřadni síň), the former mortuary, now devoted to an exhibition on illness, death and cemeteries in the Jewish tradition.

Clementinum★★
(Klementinum)

Entrances at Křižovnické náměstí 4, Karlova 1 and Mariánské náměstí 5, Old Town. Metro A: Staroměstská. 221 663 111. www.nkp.cz. The Clementinum is currently under construction, so access is limited and opening times vary.

The second-largest architectural complex of the city after Prague Castle, the Clementinum was built by the Jesuits and today serves as an outpost of the National Library. The building's most impressive façade is that of

Clementinum

the west wing, along Křižovnická street. Built by Francesco Caratti in 1653, it displays a series of monumental pillars and statues of Roman emperors. Also included in the complex are the exquisite **Baroque Library★★★**; the splendid 1724 **Chapel of Mirrors★**, which hosts regular concerts; and the **Church of St. Salvator★** *(see Religious Sites).* The observatory (the first weather observatory in the Czech lands), was where Johannes Kepler studied the laws of planetary motion. For a splendid view of the city, climb the 172 steps up to the top of the observatory's 52m/170.6ft-high **Astronomical Tower** *(hours vary; 190 Kč).*

Old Town Bridge Tower★★
(Staroměstská mostecká věž)

Old Town end of Charles Bridge at Křižovnické náměstí, Old Town. Metro A: Staroměstská. Open daily Apr–Sept 10am–10pm, Oct & Mar 10am–8pm, Nov–Feb 10am–6pm. 70 Kč.

One of Prague's many striking towers, this one is associated with Charles Bridge. The two share a physical foundation, and the imposing sandstone tower, completed in 1380, is one of Europe's finest examples of the High Gothic style. Originally, the tower was intended for defense; at the end of the Thirty Years' War, the western wall was severely damaged by Swedish cannons. Facing the tower from Charles Square (Křižovnické náměstí), you can see statues of **Charles IV★**, Wenceslas IV and St. Vitus, as well as other saints. The interior levels used to contain a guardhouse as well as a jail for wealthy debtors.

House at the Three Ostriches★
(Dům U tří pštrosů)

U Lužického Semináře 76, Lesser Town. Metro A: Malostranská. 257 288 888. www.utripstrosu.cz.

Now a hotel with 18 elegantly appointed rooms, this house was completed in 1597 by Jan Fuchs, the official supplier of ostrich feathers to the royal court, who ordered the façade paintings from which the building gets its name. Located on the winding streets

HISTORIC SITES

79

The Defenestrations of Prague

Throwing a politician out of a window is one way of taking matters into your own hands, and that has happened several times in Prague's history. These events are known as the defenestrations of Prague. The first took place in 1419, when an angry mob of Hussites, led by Jan Žižka, stormed the New Town Hall on Charles Square and threw 15 councilors out the window. Then in 1618, an angry mob of Protestants threw three regents out of a window at Prague Castle, an incident that helped trigger the Thirty Years' War. In the latter case, the men survived the 21m/70ft drop, thanks to a pile of horse manure.

of Lesser Town, just off Charles Bridge, the House at the Three Ostriches saw its first days in the hospitality industry in 1714, when an Armenian merchant opened a coffeehouse here.

House of the Golden Ring★
(Dům U Zlatého prstenu)

Týnská 6, Old Town. Metro B: Náměstí Republiky. Open year-round Tue–Sun 10am–6pm. Closed Mon. 120 Kč. 224 827 022. www.ghmp.cz.

Originally two separate medieval buildings that were subsequently joined, the House of the Golden Ring dates to the13C. Today its rooms contain a permanent collection of **20C Czech art** belonging to the City Gallery of Prague. The building's interior is worth a visit in itself for its Gothic cellars and 15C wall paintings.

New Town Hall★
(Novoměstská radnice)

Karlovo náměstí 23, New Town. Metro B: Karlovo náměstí. Rooms accessible during temporary exhibitions Tue–Sun 10am–6pm. Tower open Tue–Sun 10am–6pm. Closed Mon. 50 Kč. 224 948 229. www.nrpraha.cz.

With its high towers, this building dominates the north side of Charles Square. In spite of restoration work, the building, which in 1419 was the scene of the first defenestration of Prague *(see sidebar, opposite)*, has maintained a large number of its original Gothic-style interior elements. The tower is worth a detour for the **view★** it affords over Prague – but you'll have to climb 221 steps to enjoy it!

Old Town Hall★
(Staroměstska radnice)

Staroměstské náměstí 1/3, Old Town. Metro A: Staroměstská. Halls open year-round Mon 11am–6pm, Tue–Sun 9am–6pm; tower open Mon 11am–10pm, Tue–Sun 9am–10pm. 100 Kc. 724 508 584. www.prazskeveze.cz.

Old Town got the go-ahead for its own Town Hall in 1138, and the building was dedicated in 1364. The Hall's 70m/229.5ft tower is one of Prague's most notable sights, in particular for the famous **Astronomical Clock★★★** *(see Architectural Landmarks)*. The building next to the tower includes an **overhanging chapel★**, dating from the mid-14C. During WWII, the Town Hall was badly damaged, and part of it was

Old Town Hall

©Prague Information Service

destroyed; note the existing Town Hall's jagged edges marking where the rest once stood. Significant reconstruction yielded façades with a harmonious mix of Gothic and Renaissance designs. Next door, the **House at the Minute**★(U minutia) dates from 1611 and was home to Franz Kafka's family for seven years. It became part of the Old Town Hall in 1896. Today, the Town Hall, adorned with magnificent 17C sgraffiti, is used purely for ceremonial purposes. The city's main tourism office is located on the ground floor. From the top of the tower, a gallery offers a breathtaking **view**★★.

Powder Tower★
(Prašná brana)

Intersection of Celetná and Na Příkopě, Old Town. Metro B: Náměstí Republiky. Open Apr–Sept 10am–10pm, Oct & Mar 10am–8pm, Nov–Feb 10am–6pm. 70 Kč.

Built in the mid-13C, the Powder Tower formed part of the 11C Powder Gate attached to the original Gothic fortifications for the city's Old Town. It quickly abandoned its defensive functions and was used to store gunpowder, giving the tower its name. Partially destroyed by the Prussians in 1757, the tower was renovated in 1875; the numerous modifications carried out by **Josef Mocker** gave the structure a Gothic Revival appearance – especially the spires on the roof. Today the tower marks the beginning of the **Royal Route**, indicated by brass markings on the cobbles *(see Ideas and Tours)*. From the top, you can take in a **view**★

U Prince

One of the best views of Prague is from above, looking out over the canopy of red-tile roofs. The hotel **U Prince** *(www.hotel uprince.com)* on Old Town Square, across from the **Old Town Hall**★, has an incredible rooftop terrace *(open year-round and covered in winter)* that overlooks the bustling square and out over Old Town. Pass on the food here, but do treat yourself to a cocktail as you drink in the view.

Fit for a King

Náměstí Republiky 5. Old Town. Metro B: Náměstí Republiky. 222 002 101. www.obecni-dum.cz. The grand **Municipal House★★★** *(see Architectural Landmarks)* on Republic Square has played an important role in the Czech national identity – long before the current building was conceptualized. In the late 14C, Wenceslas IV decreed that his residence, named King's Court, be built in a strategic location next to the **Powder Tower Gate**. Later, under the rule of Vladislav II, the official royal residence was moved to Prague Castle, and King's Court fell into disuse. Shortly after the residence was demolished at the turn of the 20C, the Prague Civic Society proposed erecting a modern building here, to represent the advancements made in previous decades during the **Czech National Revival**. To this day, Municipal House exemplifies Czech cultural aspiration, and its stately rooms host visiting dignitaries and cultural events.

of the city; while on the third floor, an **exhibit** presents the various towers of Prague to the present day.

Rudolfinum★

Alšovo nábřeží 12, Josefov. Metro A: Staroměstská. See Performing Arts.

One of Prague's grandest Renaissance Revival buildings, the Rudolfinum presides over Jan Palach Square in Josefov and was designed by Josef Schulz and Josef Zítek – the same architects who designed the **National Theater** *(see Performing Arts)* – and finished in 1884. During the period between the World Wars, this palatial building was used as the seat of the Czechoslovak Parliament.

Today the Rudolfinum is home to the **Czech Philharmonic Orchestra** as well as the **Galerie Rudolfinum** *(see sidebar, opposite),* which welcomes temporary and permanent exhibitions of both modern and classical art.

Rudolfinum

©Prague Information Service

MUST SEE

Vyšehrad Fortress★
(Vyšehrad národní kulturni památka)

V. Pevnosti 159/5b, Vyšehrad. Metro C: Vyšehrad or Trams 3, 16, 17 or 21 to Výtoň. Open Apr–Oct daily 9:30am–6pm; rest of the year 9:30am–5pm. 50Kč. 241 410 348. www.praha-vysehrad.cz.

To the south of the city center, the rocky Vyšehrad Fortress once defended the approach to Prague. At the end of the Thirty Years' War in 1648, Count Raymond Montecucoli submitted a plan to fortify Prague, with Vyšehrad as its citadel. The fortress was completed in the 1720s, after which time walls were erected around the city center. After the siege of Prague by the Prussians in 1757, new fortresses were built in Josefov and Terezin, and Vyšehrad ultimately lost its status as a key defense point. Today, the fort's **Brick Gate** contains an exhibit *(20 Kč)* recalling site's long history. You can walk almost all the way around the original **ramparts** to enjoy the splendid views.

Below the castle, on the corner of Vinislavova and de Rašínovo nábřeží, as well as on Neklanová, note the series of **Cubist houses★**, a style that was all the rage in Prague between 1911 and 1914.

Carolinum
(Karolinum)

Ovocný trh 3, Old Town. Metro A or B: Můstek. Not open to the public. 224 491 326. www.cuni.cz.

This is the seat of the oldest university in Central Europe, Charles University, which was established by Charles IV in 1348, and today has facilities around the city. Outside, the original Gothic architecture was entirely reworked in the Baroque style in the 18C. Inside, numerous original decorations have survived but are unfortunately not accessible. Today, the Carolinum houses the university's administrative offices, although occasionally the building hosts temporary exhibits that allow a glimpse of the interior.

Church of Sts. Cyril and Methodius
(Sv. Cyrila a Metoděje)

Corner of Resslova 9a, New Town. Metro B: Karlovo náměstí. Open: Apr–Oct Tue–Sun 10am–5pm, Nov–March 10am–4pm. 60 Kč. 224 920 686. www.pravoslavnacirkev.cz.

Apart from its role as a mainstay of the Czech Orthodox Church, the Baroque Church of Sts. Cyril and Methodius played a dramatic role in World War II. A small group of Czech paratroopers, trained by the British RAF, carried out the assassination of Nazi Reichsprotektor Reinhardt Heydrich in 1942. A search for the assassins led to a standoff outside

---

Galerie Rudolfinum

Open Tue–Sun 10am–6pm. www.galerierudolfinum.cz/en. In addition to being a prestigious performance space, the **Rudolfinum★** also houses an art gallery. **Galerie Rudolfinum**, associated with the Museum of Decorative Arts *(see Museums)*, hosts rotating exhibits of contemporary and international photos, prints and paintings.

The Parachutists

After hearing about the last moments of Heydrich's assassins in the **Church of Sts. Cyril and Methodius** *(see p83)*, visit the U Parašutistů pub across the street *(Resslova 7)*, which is dedicated to the Czech heroes. Walls here are covered in newspaper clippings, photographs of the men and other memorabilia from that fateful day in 1942. While it's a sobering story to contemplate, the pub does have excellent Pilsner on tap and cheap, hearty Czech fare.

this church, where the seven paratroopers were barricaded in the crypt. The church now honors this piece of history in the **National Memorial to the Heroes of the Heydrich Terror** (Národní památník obětí heydrichiády; *enter under the exterior stairway; same hours as church; 60 Kč*). where exhibits limn the events leading up to the paratroopers' suicides. Outside the church, bullet holes

still pockmark the stone walls and a recently erected marble monument lists the names of 294 local patriots who were killed during the Nazis' vengeful crackdown.

Jewish Town Hall
(Židovská radnice)

Maiselova 18, Josefov. Tram 17: Právnická fakulta. Not open to the public. 221 714 444.

Next to the picturesque **Old-New Synagogue★★★** *(see Religious Sites)*, this Rococo Town Hall was rebuilt in the 18C, replacing the Renaissance structure from 1586. The **tower**, crowned with a Star of David, features a conventional clock with four faces; above, on the gable, notice the clock face with Hebrew characters. The hands turn counterclockwise to allow the Hebrew to be read in the right direction. Today, the Town Hall still fulfills its original function as the center of the Jewish community in Prague. It is also the seat of the head rabbi, and contains a library and a meeting hall.

Olšany Cemeteries

©Shaun Higson/age fotostock

Jindřišská Tower
(Jindřišská věž)

*Jindřišská, **New Town**. Metro A or B: Můstek. Open daily year-round 10am–7pm. 224 232 429. Entry 80 Kč.*

At 10 stories, Jindřišská Tower ranks as Prague's highest separate belfry, and the gallery on the top floor affords unbeatable views over New Town. Just steps from Wenceslas Square, the tower was completed in 1476 in the late Gothic style, and underwent several renovations over the centuries before being treated to a complete reconstruction that ended in 2002. The tower now features an exhibit on the towers of Prague, a pricey but pretty restaurant and a whisky bar. An elevator whisks visitors nearly to the top, leaving just 14 steps to climb by foot.

Lesser Town Bridge Towers
(Malostranské mostecké věže)

Lesser Town end of Charles Bridge. Metro A: Malostranská. Open daily Apr–Sept 10am–10pm, Oct & Mar 10am–8pm, Nov–Feb 10am–6pm. 70 Kč.

Each of these two very different towers has its own history. The smaller of the two dates from the 12C, even before the construction of Charles Bridge, and is known as the Judith Tower (named after the stone Judith Bridge, which preceded today's span). It retains its Romanesque look and was used as a jail for more than 200 years. The larger tower was built in 1357. Climb to the top of either tower for great **views★★** of the city.

Jindřišská Tower

©Peter Erik Forsberg/age fotostock

A bridged gate (early 15C) connects the two structures, and it's not uncommon to see a court herald in period costume trumpeting from the top.

Olšany Cemeteries
(Olšanské hřbitovy)

*Vinohradská 2807, **Vinohrady**. Trams 5, 10, 11 or 16: Olšanské hřbitovy. Open May–Sept 8am–9pm, Mar–Apr & Oct 8am–6pm, Nov–Feb 9am–4pm. 267 310 652.*

This sprawling complex of 12 cemeteries, comprising the largest necropolis in the country, was built in 1680 to accommodate Prague plague victims. Over the course of its existence, more than 2 million people have been buried here. Today it is a peaceful park – replete with twisting, ancient boughs, ivy-covered gravestones and Art Nouveau-style monuments. Many politicians and celebrities lie here; the **Olšany Cemetery Learning Trail** marks an informative route through three of the 12 cemeteries.

HISTORIC SITES

85

MUSEUMS

In many ways, Prague itself is a living, breathing museum, a permanent and continuously evolving testament to the city's history. Beyond that, Prague supports a rich tradition of museums, where culture lovers will discover everything from fine art to astronomy.

Convent of St. Agnes of Bohemia: National Gallery of Medieval Art★★★
(Klášter sv. Anežky České-Národní galerie)

*U milosrdných 17, **Old Town**. Metro B: Náměstí Republiky. Open Tue–Sun 10am–6pm. Closed Mon. 150 Kč. 224 810 628. www.ngprague.cz.*

This convent was founded in the 13C by Princess Agnes, the daughter of Otakar I and sister of the future ruler Wenceslas I. Closed in 1782 by Joseph II, it was no more than a ruin at the end of the 19C and came very close to being destroyed; its restoration would take a century to achieve. It now provides a magnificent space for the **exhibition of Medieval Art in Bohemia and Central Europe**. The paintings, sculptures, liturgical art and more displayed in the rooms of the convent date from

the 12C to 16C and come from the Czech Republic, Slovakia and Germany. Don't miss the collection of 14C and 15C **Madonnas**, and the handful of works by Cranach the Elder.

Trade Fair Palace: Museum of Modern and Contemporary Art★★★
(Veletržní palác – Muzeum moderního a současného umění)

*Dukelských hrdinů 47, **Holešovice**. Tram 5, 12, 14 or 17: Veletržní. Open Tue–Sun 10am–6pm. Closed Mon. 250 Kč. 224 301 122. www.ngprague.cz.*

For more than 10 years, this Functionalist **palace★** north of the city center has displayed the largest collection of the **Prague National Gallery**, focusing on modern and contemporary art of the 19C and 20C.

Convent of St. Agnes of Bohemia

MUST SEE

Trade Fair Palace

©Nick Servian/age fotostock

(1884-1918), one of the great names in Czech Cubism.

Head for the fourth floor to see **19C art★**, where the well-curated collection encompasses works by Czech Romantic painter **Alfons Mucha**, and an immense collection of paintings by Mánes, Kosárek, Pinkas and Slaviček. Sculptures by Myslbek complete the portrait of this generation of artists, who have all contributed to the building or decoration of the great monuments of Prague. Temporary installations fill the fifth floor.

The first floor is dedicated to **foreign 20C art★**, while the second floor displays **Czech art from 1930 to the present day★** – in particular works by **František Janoušek**, the founder of the Surrealism movement in Czechoslovakia. In the section on photography, note the prints by **Josef Koudelka**, who won the Robert Capa Gold Medal Award in 1969 for his photographs depicting Soviet tanks entering Prague. On the third floor, you'll find an interesting collection of **French art from the 19C and 20C★★**, including Rodin, Delacroix and Picasso. However, the most interesting is the section on **Czech art from 1900 to 1930★★** including **František Kupka** (1871-1957) and his depictions of the world's big cities; and the excellent paintings by **Bohumil Kubišta**

Kampa Museum: The Jan and Meda Mládek Foundation★★
(Muzeum Kampa - nadace Jana a Medy Mládkových)

U Sovových mlýnů 503/2, Lesser Town. Trams 12, 20 or 22: Hellichova. Open daily 10am–6pm. 260 Kč. 257 286 147. www.museumkampa.cz.

While in exile in the US during the Communist regime in Czechoslovakia, Jan and Meda Mládek gathered significant collections of Czech art of the 20C. They supported young artists, notably by purchasing the works of persecuted artists who were banned from exhibiting. After amassing an impressive collection, the couple donated it to the city of

Museum Night

Once a year, Prague's museums are open to the public free of charge until late in the evening. Called **Prague Museum Night**, the annual event takes place on the second Saturday of June, and nearly all of the city's museums participate. Organized by the **National Museum★** in cooperation with Prague public transit, the event provides buses (also free of charge) that ferry folks between the museums.

A New Look in 3-D

The best exhibit at the **Museum of the City of Prague★★** has long been artist Anton Langweil's scale model of 18C Prague; and now, with an interactive 3-D video, it's even better. Wearing the 3-D glasses provided, you are swept into the alleys and streets of the model itself, letting you appreciate the awesome detail of the model's creation and get a feel for what life was like in Prague more than two centuries ago.

which retraces the development of the city from prehistoric times to the 18C, explaining how the distinct areas of Prague eventually came together to form one city. Here, too, is the original **face** painted by Mikoláš Aleš for the **Astronomical Clock★★★** *(see Architectural Landmarks).* However, the big attraction here is the **model of Prague★**. It took **Anton Langweil** eight years (1826–1834) to complete this project. On a scale of 1/148, the model covers about 20m²/215sq ft and shows the Lesser Town and Hradčany at the dawn of the Industrial Age.

Prague, where it is now on display at the Kampa Museum. Emphasis is given to current Czech art with a fine selection of contemporary works by living artists.

Museum of the City of Prague★★
(Muzeum hlavního města Prahy)

Na Poříčí 52, Florenc. Metro B or C: Florenc. Open Tue–Sun 9am–6pm. Closed Mon. 120 Kč. 224 816 772. www.museumprahy.cz.

This splendid Renaissance Revival palace houses one of the best collections of pieces relating to the daily life of Prague residents and the development of the city over the centuries. Begin by admiring the building itself, the work of the architect **Antonín Wiehl**, who also designed the tomb of Slavín in the **Vyšehrad Slavín Cemetery** *(see Parks and Gardens).* Inside, the **staircase★**, divided into three parts, displays a superb panoramic fresco of Prague in 1896. Seek out the **exhibition on the history of Prague★★**,

National Technical Museum★★
(Národní technické muzeum)

Kostelní 42, Letná. Trams 1, 8, 15, 25 or 26: Letenské náměstí. Open Tue–Sun 10am–6pm (first Thu of the month until 8pm). Closed Mon. 170 Kč. 220 399 111. www.ntm.cz.

Set back from the east side of Letná Park, this 1942 Functionalist building houses collections representing various aspects of science and technology as well as the contribution of the Czech nation to these fields. It reopened recently after a renovation, and now, in addition to its 5,000 fascinating exhibits, the museum features a **Supermarine Spitfire fighter jet** from 1945. Of the original exhibits, **The Measurement of Time** shows off a fabulous variety of objects, from sun dials to digital clocks. **Interkamera** presents 2,500 pieces illustrating the history of photography and films. In the same spirit, the second floor is dedicated to **acoustics**,

MUST SEE

from the first slot-fed record players to jukeboxes. The third floor celebrates **astronomy**, with a fascinating collection of instruments used by astronomer Tycho Brahe in the 16C. In the basement, a 1km/0.6mi-long **mine shaft** has been re-created along with the antique and modern tools and machines used to extract minerals from the earth.

Sternberg Palace – National Gallery★★
(Šternberský paláca – národní galerie)

Hradčanské náměstí 15, Hradčany. Tram 22: Pražský hrad. Open Tue–Sun 10am–6pm. Closed Mon. 150 Kč. 223 090 570. www.ngprague.cz.

Built between 1698 and 1707 for Count **Kaspar Maria von Sternberg** by Italian architect Giovanni Battista Alliprandi, the palace is arranged around a spacious interior courtyard. His residence was the first permanent residence of The National Gallery in 1819. Today, the gallery contains a rich collection of paintings by European masters, especially German and Flemish painters.

The first level is dedicated to the medieval period, with paintings dating from the 14C to the 16C, including a rare group of Italian primitives. Flemish painting is represented by triptychs and several remarkable works by **Jan Gossaert**, also known as Mabuse. Find German and Italian Renaissance paintings on the second floor. The German collection is extremely rich, with notable works by **Cranach the Elder** and **Dürer**. Don't forget to look up at the ceiling, especially in the Antique Room, decorated by Johann Rudolf Bys. In the north wing, you'll see several masterpieces by **Rubens** and **Rembrandt**.

Bedřich Smetana Museum★
(Muzeum Bedřicha Smetany)

Novotného lávka 1, Old Town. Metro A: Staroměstská. Open Wed–Mon 10am–5pm, closed Tue. 50 Kč. 222 220 082. www.nm.cz.

Located in the former Old Town Water Tower, this little museum retraces the life of the famous composer of "My Country"

Bedřich Smetana Museum

©National Museum

(Má Vlast), **Bedřich Smetana** (1824–84) through a large collection of the composer's correspondence and personal objects. The museum's windows offer views over the first few arches of the **Charles Bridge★★★**.

Czech Museum of Music – Collection of Musical Instruments★
(České muzeum hudby– muzeum hudebních nástroju)

Karmelitská 2/4, Lesser Town. Tram 12, 20 or 22 Hellichova. Open Wed–Mon 10am–6pm. Closed Tue. 100 Kč (free the first Thu of every month). 257 257 777. www.nm.cz.

Music-loving Prague now has a museum worthy of its passion. Located in a Baroque palace built by Italian architect Francesco Caratti in the 17C, the exhibition presents the history of music and musical instruments from the 16C to the 21C. Pieces on display show off an incredible quality, and most

Czech Museum of Music

©National Museum

are accompanied by soundtracks allowing you to hear their sounds. The collection also encompasses rare instruments, such as a synthesizer dating from 1956.

Dvořák Museum★
(Muzeum Antinína Dvořáka)

Ke Karlovu 20, New Town. Metro C: I.P. Pavlova. Open Apr–Sep Tue–Sun 10am–1:30pm & 2pm–5pm; Thu 11am–3:30pm & 4pm–7pm; Oct–Mar Tue–Sun 10am–1:30pm & 2pm–5pm. 50 Kc. 224 923 363.

Hidden in a Baroque **villa★** (designed by Kilián Ignác Dientzenhofer in 1720) in the south part of the New Town, the Dvořák Museum brings to life the music and personal effects of the much-loved Czech composer and passionate observer of America **Antonin Dvořák** (1841–1904). Part of the Czech Museum of Music, the museum hosts exhibits of the composer's sheet music manuscripts and correspondence. Concerts of Dvořák's music are held here in a lovely room decorated with frescoes.

Museum of Czech Cubism★
(Muzeum českého kubismu)

Ovocný trh 19, Old Town. Metro B: Námesti Republiky. Open Tue–Sun 10am–6pm, 100 Kč. 222 310 481. www.ngprague.cz.

Contained on the second and third floors of the **House of the Black Madonna★**, this collection includes objects from the turn of the 20C, showing how the national artistic sensibility took off with the creation of Rondo-Cubism.

MUST SEE

Paintings, drawings, ceramics, furniture and designs by artists such as Otto Gutfreund and Emil Filla are on view. Check out the ground-floor gift shop for replicas of some of the exhibited items *(see sidebar, opposite)*.

Museum of Decorative Arts★
(Uměleckoprůmyslové muzeum)

Listopadu 2, Josefov. Tram 17: Pravnicka fakulta. Open Tue 10am–7pm, Wed 10am–6pm. 120 Kč. 251 093 111. www.upm.cz.

Built in 1898, this palace houses the Museum of Decorative Arts, which presents tapestries, lace, porcelain, clothing, glassware, clocks and more items, covering the years from medieval times to the beginning of the 20C. The vast majority of pieces come from the Czech Republic or Central Europe.

National Museum★
(Národní museum)

Václavské náměstí 68, New Town. Metro A or C: Muzeum. Main building closed for renovation. 224 497 111. www.nm.cz.

On **Wenceslas Square★★★** *(see Historic Squares)*, where one of the gateways to the city once stood, the imposing National Museum now rises against the backdrop to the busy boulevard. Although the museum is currently closed for reconstruction and slated to reopen in June 2015, you can still see the building's exterior, one of Prague's iconic images. The National Museum took shape in the 19C as the pet project of Count **Kaspar Maria von Sternberg**

National Museum

©Ing. Pavel Dosoudil

to present the scientific and historical riches of Bohemia. Built in 1885 expressly to display all the collections, the building, designed by architect **Josef Schultz** in the Renaissance Revival style, opened to the public five years later. While the museum undergoes a needed facelift, temporary exhibits are being shown next door at the former **Radio Free Europe/Radio Liberty building** *(Vinohradská 1, New Town; open daily 10am–6pm; first Wed of the month until 8pm; closed the first Tue of the month; 224 497 111; 60 Kč).*

Gallery Kubista

Ovocný trh 19, Old Town. Same hours as museum. www.kubista.cz
The shop in the **Museum of Czech Cubism★** sells ceramics, glass, metal goods, textiles and a host of other objects from the Art Deco and Cubist periods. You'll also find numerous books on Cubism, with a special focus on the Czech contribution of Rondo-Cubism.

MUSEUMS

Flogging a Dead Horse

In 1999, an ambitious project to take art out of museums and into non-gallery spaces was unleashed in Prague. Housed in spaces such as an abandoned print works on Wenceslas Square, **99CZ** looked at Czech art's evolution in the decade since Communism. Sculptor **David Černý's** contribution hung at the foot of Wenceslas Square, facing Myslbek's **Statue of St. Wenceslas**, and mirroring every detail bar one: Černý's nag was upside down and dead, tongue lolling. It was intended as a criticism of President Václav Havel, who was in a dispute with his sister-in-law over the Lucerna Palace. After 99CZ disappeared, Černý's take on the patron saint reappeared, this time in the arcade of **Lucerna Palace★★** *(Vodičkova 36, New Town; Metro A or B: Můstek; see Performing Arts)*, where it is displayed today.

Czech Museum of Fine Arts
(České Muzeum Výtvarných umění)

Husova 19–21, Old Town. Metro A: Staroměstská. Open Tue–Sun 10am–6pm. Closed Mon. 50 Kč. 222 220 218. www.cmvu.cz.

While this museum has several branches around the city, this location in Old Town is its headquarters. The collection was first exhibited in the 1960s, and moved between several towns and buildings as it attempted to dodge the repressive authorities. Today, the collection spans the artistic development of Czech art over the course of the 20C, from neo-Romanticism through Art Nouveau and Symbolism to Czech Modernism.

DOX/Centre for Contemporary Art
(Centrum současného umění)

Poupětova 1, Holešovice. Metro C: Holešovice. Open Sun–Mon 10am–6pm, Wed–Fri 11am–7pm. Closed Tue. 180 Kč. 224 930 927. www.doxprague.org.

The objective of this hip gallery, located in a former industrial site reworked by Ivan Kroupa, is to display contemporary **Czech art** in an international context. Sculptures, videos, paintings, photographs and architecture are brought together here in provocative **temporary exhibits** that encourage thinking outside the box. The museum's **Designshop** will attract lovers of original objects.

DOX/Centre for Contemporary Art

©DOX/Centre for Contemporary Art

Franz Kafka Museum

Cihelná 2b, Lesser Town. Metro A: Malostranská. Open daily 10am–6pm. 180 Kč. 221 451 333. www.kafkamuseum.cz.

Celebrating the life and work of the famous Czech writer **Franz Kafka** (1883–1924), exhibits at the museum examine Kafka's relationship to the city of Prague and the influence that this relationship had on his career. The first part of the permanent exhibit conjures up Kafka's daily life and surroundings: his birthplace; his family relationships – especially with his father; and the influence that Jewish and German-language literary circles had on his work. In the second part, letters, photographs and first editions of his work illustrate his writing method and the effects that his stuttering, his day job, and his various mistresses all had on his work.

Mucha Museum
(Muchovo museum)

Panská 7, New Town. Metro A or B: Můstek. Open daily 10am–6pm. 160 Kč. 224 216 415. www.mucha.cz.

Renowned for his turn-of-the-19C style, Czech Romantic painter

Alfons Mucha (1860–1939) is often considered alongside the masters of the Parisian Art Nouveau style – even though Mucha was born in Moravia. The museum named for him is housed in the Baroque Kaunický Palace and contains more than 100 of Mucha's paintings, photos, drawings, pastels and lithographs, from his famous depictions of Sarah Bernhardt to his lesser-known prints.

Museum of Communism
(Muzeum Komunismu)

Na Příkopě 10, New Town. Metro A or B Můstek. Open daily 9am–9pm. 180 Kč. 224 212 966. www.muzeumkomunismu.cz.

Rooms in this museum display, in no particular order, educational and anecdotal objects and documents – telephones, posters, packaging and other products "made in Communism." In a little room at the back, you can watch interesting documentaries and archival images recounting Prague's days under Communism, from the coup in 1948 to the regime's collapse in 1989.

Slav Epic

While **Alfons Mucha**'s Art Nouveau posters are instantly recognizable, the Czech painter's true masterpiece remains relatively unknown. Called *The Slav Epic*, it comprises 20 large-scale panels that depict the history of the Czech nation and the Slavic people. Mucha worked on it for years, and left it to the city of Prague in 1928. Many repressive regimes and legal disputes later, the series has finally returned to Prague, and is now on view at the **Trade Fair Palace: Museum of Modern and Contemporary Art★★★** *(see p86)*.

MUSEUMS

PARKS AND GARDENS

If you're feeling a bit cobble-eyed from pounding the pavement around Prague's alleyways, and if the temperamental Prague weather is shining in your favor, take some time out from gazing upon frescoes cloistered in dark rooms and explore the city's rich array of breathtaking parks and gardens. These range from English-style lawns and statue-studded greenswards to relaxed urban spaces ideal for a picnic with a bottle of wine, or just a breather before moving on to the next sight. Prague has an enviable amount of green space, and it is in these places that one can truly breathe in the city's *joie de vivre*.

MUST SEE

Gardens Below Prague Castle★★★
(Zahrady pod Pražským hradem)

Lesser Town. Enter through Valdštejnské náměstí 3/162 and through the castle's southern gardens. Metro A: Malostranská. Open daily Jun–Jul 10am–9pm; Aug daily 10am–8pm; rest of the year, hours vary. 80 Kč. 257 010 401. www.palacovezahrady.cz.

These terraced gardens that descend in dainty step to Lesser Town provide a respite from the crowds that hover around Prague Castle. The series of gardens is flanked on one side by the walls to the **Wallenstein Gardens★★** and on the other by a series of Baroque palaces that today house international embassies and government ministries. A beautiful late-17C *sala terrena* designed by František Maximilián Kaňka is the focal point of the **Ledebour Garden**. A double staircase climbs the terraces up to a little pavilion at the foot of the castle wall. From there you have an unobstructed view over the red-tiled roofs of the Lesser Town and the famed spires of the city of Prague.

Winding your way east through the gardens, you'll come across **Pálffy Garden**, with its central staircase and tunnel, then **Kolowrat Garden** with its elevated pavilion, or gloriette.

Ledebour Garden

©Prague Information Service

Old Castle Steps★★ (Zámecké schody)

Prague Castle's hilltop location is great for the views, but it can be a tiring climb up countless steps. To save your soles for further sightseeing, arrive at the castle by tram, and then take the Old Castle Steps down to the Malostranská metro station. The gradual, cobbled descent of 121 steps affords lush vistas over both the city and of the **South Gardens★★** of **Prague Castle★★★**.

Prague Castle South Gardens★★
(Jižní zahrady)

Hradčany. Entrances: inside the castle through the third courtyard (Bull Staircase); from the west by the New Castle Stairs); or from the east by the Old Castle Stairs. Metro A: Malostranská. Open daily Jun–Jul 10am–9pm, Aug 10am–8pm; rest of the year, hours vary. Closed in winter. 224 371 111. www.hrad.cz.

Running all along Prague castle, this series of gardens offers splendid views of the cityscape. In the 1920s, Josip Plečnik, the castle architect, strove to make the gardens more harmonious with their surroundings.
To the west, **Paradise Garden** (Rajská zahrada) was created in 1562 by Archduke Ferdinand. Farther east are the **Gardens on the Ramparts** (Zahrady na valech); on the other side of a colonnaded gazebo, at the bottom of the staircase, **Hartig Garden** (Hartigovská zahrada) occupies a Baroque music pavilion.
Near the east entrance, a column topped with a gilded sphere streaked with lightning bolts stands above the **Moravian Bastion** (Moravská bašta). From here, stairs provide access to the **Gardens Below Prague Castle★★★**.

Royal Gardens★★
(Královská zahrada)

Hradčany. Enter from inside Prague Castle through the second courtyard; from the north by U Prašného mostu; or from the east by Mariánské hradby. Tram 22: Prazsky most. Open Jun–Jul daily 10am–9pm; Aug 10am–8pm; rest of the year, hours vary. Closed in winter. 224 371 111. www.hrad.cz.

The Royal Gardens were developed under the reigns of Archduke Ferdinand and Rudolf II to accommodate rare plants and exotic animals. The first tulips in Europe bloomed in these beds, where parrots were once tethered to branches with fine golden chains. Though laid out in the formal French style, the plantings today follow a more natural design.

Vrtba Garden★★
(Vrtbovská zahrada)

Karmelitská 25, Lesser Town. Trams 12, 20 or 22: Hellichova. Open Apr–Oct 10am–6pm. 55 Kč. 272 088 350. www.vrtbovska.cz.

Don't miss the hidden corner of heaven that is the Baroque garden of Vrtba Palace. After undergoing a long restoration, the garden and palace were finally opened again to the public. Both are the work of architect František Maximilián

Kaňka, who converted a former Renaissance house into this large Baroque palace. The terraced gardens sit alongside Petřín Hill, offering lovely, peaceful **views★★** across the red roofs of the Lesser Town.

Wallenstein Gardens★★
(Valdstejnská zahrada)

Valdstejnská 3 and Klárov, Lesser Town. Metro A: Malostranská. Open daily Apr–Oct 10am–6 pm. 257 072 759.

The clever layout of this garden, with its geometrical flower beds and hedged-in walkways, makes it seem more extensive than the actual space between its walls. The superb view that takes in Prague Castle and the cathedral enhances this effect. Dominated by the **Wallenstein Palace★** *(see Palaces)*, the west end is the most interesting and includes Pieroni's superb **sala terrena★★**, linking the garden with the palace. Beyond this stretches a path lined by two stunning rows of bronze **statues★★**, dynamic masterpieces created by Adriaen de Vries, the sculptor in Rudolf II's court. These statues are only copies, however; the originals were carried off by the Swedes in 1648.

Franciscan Gardens★
(Františkánská zahrada)

Enter on Vodičkova via the Svetozor Passage, Jungmannnovo náměstí, New Town. Metro A or B: Můstek. Open mid-Apr–mid-Sept 7am–10pm; rest of the year hours vary.

Dating back as far as the 14C, these gardens are known for their extensive rose blossoms in spring. On a sunny summer's day, nearly every bench is occupied by locals enjoying an ice cream amid the foliage and flowers. Originally part of the monastery of **Our Lady of the Snows Basilica★** *(see Religious Sites)*, the garden was opened to the public in 1950. After being reworked in 1992, it now offers a haven of tranquility away from the crowds on Wenceslas Square, and serves as a shortcut between the square and **National Avenue★** (Národní třída).

Franciscan Gardens

©Pietro Scozzari/age fotostock

🌿 Kampa Park★

Enter to the south below Charles Bridge, Lesser Town. Metro A: Malostranská.

An urban oasis, **Kampa Island** is mostly taken up by relaxed park space that forms a popular gathering point underneath the willows for couples, groups of friends, or workers on their lunch break. Charming **Na Kampě Square★★** reaches from the base

MUST SEE

of Charles Bridge to the opening of the park, which is hedged on one side by Čertovka (the Devil's Stream), an artificial reach built in medieval times to run water mills; it now separates Kampa from the Lesser Town. Outdoor art exhibitions and spontaneous concerts are often staged on the other side of the park, where you'll find a number of fancy seafood restaurants.

Letná Park★
(Letenské sady)

Letná. Prague 6. Tram 1, 8 or 15: Letenské náměstí. Open dawn until dark.

For locals, Letná Park is one of the city's true gems, a sprawling urban park north of the city center that fosters exercise on its walking and roller-blading paths, and contains several children's playgrounds. Some stellar views can be had from this park, which borders the **Letná Plain**. One of the city's best beer gardens *(see sidebar, above)* is also found here.

Rising from atop the sharp ledge that winds down toward the river is

Beer Gardens
In Prague, beer almost does grow on trees. The national drink can be found everywhere, including in many of the city's parks under the umbrellas of a beer garden – usually a series of picnic tables and a kiosk selling beer, soft drinks and snacks like hot dogs and ice cream. The beer garden in hilltop **Letná Park★** *(see Nightlife)* is the city's biggest and most popular, with priceless views over the city.

the **Metronome**, *(see Architectural Landmarks)* a feat of both artistic invention and historical significance. Adjacent to the park, **Chotek Garden** (Chotkovy sady) was planted in 1830; Franz Kafka once referred to Chotek as "the prettiest place in Prague." To the west, a **Belvedere** overlooks the garden, concealing within it a cave filled with characters from the works of the Neo-Romantic poet Julius Zeyer. **Little Hanava pavilion** (Hanavský pavilón) shows off its Baroque Revival decoration. Originally an exhibition building

Letná Park

©Rod Purcell/Apa Publications

PARKS AND GARDENS

constructed in the Duke of Hanau's foundries for the Jubilee Exhibition of 1891, the pavilion was recently converted into a pricey restaurant whose terrace offers extraordinary **views★★** of the city.

Vojan Park★
(Vojanovy sady)

*U lužického semináře 17, **Lesser Town**. Metro A: Malostranská. Open daily in summer 8am–7pm; winter 9am until dark.*

The high walls that surround this garden protect the exotic trees and shrubs within. Built as an integral part of a medieval Episcopal estate, the garden is one of Prague's earliest, dating to around the year 1300. It later became the property of the St. Joseph Carmelites, whose monastery it borders. Today it is a public park, encompassing the cave-shaped **St. Elias Chapel**, another chapel dedicated to St. Theresa, and a statue of John of Nepomuk that is built into a wall. The park maintains its original geometric shape, where peacocks roam freely. Numerous fruit trees –

free for the picking – add to its whimsical feel.

Charles University Botanical Garden

*Na slupi 16, **New Town**. Tram 18 or 24: Botanická zahrada. Open daily mid-Mar–Oct 10am–6pm; rest of the year hours vary. 50 Kč for greenhouse exhibit. 224 918 970.*

For anyone interested in multitudes of flora and fauna, or just a quiet place to take a break close to **Charles Square★** (*see Historic Squares*), the botanical garden of Charles University will be a welcome detour. In addition to secret shady nooks and gazebos, the garden features a greenhouse with a permanent exhibit of tropical and subtropical plant life. A giant gingko biloba plant, thought to be 130 years old, is one of the unique specimens.

Petřín Park
(Petřínské sady)

*Petřín Hill, **Lesser Town**. Trams 6, 9, 12 or 20: Újezd. Open daily Apr–Sept 10am–10pm, Oct–Mar 10am–8pm, Nov–Feb 10am–6pm. 257 320 112.*

Rising above the Lesser Town, the park atop Petřín Hill has a long-held reputation as a haven for lovers (*see sidebar, opposite*). The winding paths that crisscross the slope burst with cherry blossoms come spring, and while the **funicular** (*see Family Fun*) provides a quicker ascent, walking lets you take in the incredible views and see the ivy-coated Stations of the Cross along the way. If you're feeling brave, climb **Petřín Tower** (*see p111*), a 60m/197ft-tall replica

Vojan Park

©Chmura Frank/age fotostock

Statue of Karel Hynek Mácha, Petřín Park

©Prague Information Service

of the world, to impressive effect. The splendid series of **statues★★** depicts the gods of Olympia sending the Titans to hell.

Vyšehrad Gardens

V Pevnosti 159/5b, Vyšehrad. Metro C: Vyšehrad. Open daily Apr–Oct 9:30am–6pm; rest of the year daily 9:30am–5pm. 241 410 348. www.praha-vysehrad.cz.

The fortress surrounding Vyšehrad has plenty to explore within its walled fortifications, set on a hill with fantastic views over the Vltava River and the city. After marveling at the grandeur of **Vyšehrad Cathedral** *(see Religious Sites)*, check out the adjacent **Vyšehrad Slavín Cemetery** *(K Rotundé 10; open daily; hours vary seasonally)*, a beautifully tended hodge-podge of elaborately sculpted burial plots to past Czech luminaries – including artist Alfons Mucha and composers Bedřich Smetana and Antonín Dvořák. Enter the **Brick Gate** *(V Pevnosti 159/5b; open Apr–Oct 9:30am–6pm; Mar, Nov–Dec 9:30am–5pm; closed Jan–Feb; 20 Kc; 241 410 352)* to see an exhibition on the fortification's history.

of the Eiffel Tower, for a bird's-eye view, or wander through the **Rose Garden**. Children young and old will love the **Mirror Maze** *(see Family Fun)*. For the best of the best views, enter the park from the lookout next to **Strahov Monastery★★** *(see Religious Sites)*.

Troja Botanical Gardens

Nadvorni 134, Troja. Metro C: Holešovice, then bus 112 to stop Zoologická zahrada. Open daily May–Sept 9am–7pm; hours vary seasonally. 120 Kc; charges for individual exhibitions vary. 603 582 191. www.botanicka.cz.

Spread out over the hillside near the **Troja Chateau** *(see Palaces)*, Troja Botanical Gardens comprise several exhibits, both permanent and rotating seasonally. These include the Japanese Garden, the Fata Morgana tropical greenhouse, and St. Claire's Vineyard, where you can sample the local wines and look out over the city. Other sections of the gardens focus on flora and fauna from different parts

Petřín Park for Lovers

On May 1, lovers flock to Petřín Park. Honoring the legacy of the poem *Máj* (May) by the Czech Romantic poet **Karel Hynek Mácha** (1810–1836), couples meet near his statue on that day before retreating into the park for canoodling. For luck, women are supposed to be kissed under the cherry blossoms.

EXCURSIONS

You don't have to travel far into the area outside Prague to visit breathtaking natural sites, historic castles, or fairy-tale medieval towns; many places lie within an hour's journey by bus or train from the capital. Whether you choose to check out the home of the famous Pilsner Urquell beer, explore a bone church or scramble up rocks to stunning vistas, it's not hard to find a daytrip from Prague – if you can manage to decide where to go.

Brno

184km /115mi southeast of Prague. Several buses and trains depart hourly from Florenc and the main train station; approx. 2 hrs 45min.

While considerably smaller than the capital, the Czech Republic's second-largest city is full of Moravian charm and its share of historic sights, as well as pubs and restaurants. Brno's universities give the city a funky feel, especially on weekend evenings. Since Brno doesn't get the hoards of tourists that Prague does, it's a bit easier to meander the streets, see the sights at your leisure, and share a pint with the locals. **Freedom Square**, at the city center, is a good jumping-off point for exploring, while **Špilberk Castle** (*Špilberk 1; casemates open daily May–Jun*

Touring Tip

For details of train and/or bus connections, visit the website **www.idos.cz** (available in English). The bus company Student Agency (*www.studentagency. cz*) also has good fares to many destinations.

10am–5pm, Jul–Sept 10am–6pm, Oct–Apr Tue–Sun 9am–5pm; 542 123 615; www.spilberk.cz) dominates the skyline.

Český Krumlov

Approx. 161km/100mi south of Prague. Buses depart every two hours from Prague's Florenc station, approx. 3hrs.

It's not hard to see why this picture-perfect medieval town, a

Špilberk Castle, Brno

©matteuss/iStockphoto

MUST SEE

Dining Out In Český Krumlov

After touring the fairy-tale chateau, try the local Eggenberg beer, served at most places around town, and book ahead for a medieval feast at **Krčma Šatlavské ulici** *(Tavern on Šatlava Street; Horní 157; 380 713 344; www.satlava.cz)*, a brick-lined cellar where top-quality meats are grilled over a huge open fire in the main dining room.

UNESCO World Heritage Site near the Austrian border, gets so packed with tourists come summer each year. Its candy-colored Renaissance **chateau** *(Zámek 59; open Tue–Sun April–May & Sept–Oct 9am–5pm; June–Aug 9am– 6pm; closed Mon; www.castle.ckrumlov.cz; 380 704 711)* and English gardens are a lovely place to spend an afternoon. The tiny, cobbled streets of the town itself – surrounded on three sides by the Vltava River – are perfect for wandering. The castle comprises four main parts: the castle itself, the theater, the museum and the lapidarium. From mid-July to late August, Krumlov plays host to the **International Music Festival Český Krumlov**, which puts on baroque and classical concerts in parks and other venues around town.

Czech Paradise
(Český raj)

Approx. 97 km/60mi northeast of Prague in near Jičín. Buses depart hourly from the Černý most station; approx. 1.5hrs. www.cesky-raj.info.

For a true excursion into some of the Czech Republic's most beautiful landscapes, Czech Paradise lives up to its name. This sprawling national park, a UNESCO protected area, covers about 200km²/77sq mi. It is famous for its so-called rock cities, natural formations of sandstone,

as well as the craggy rocks that jut out above the pine forests; be sure to see the **Hrubá skála rocks** and the **Prachovské skála rocks**. These rocks are a popular destination for local climbers, and the park's rolling landscape is ideal for hikes and bike rides, as well as cross-country skiing in winter. Other must-sees include the **castle ruins of Trosky** *(open Apr & Oct Sun, Mon & holidays 8:30am–4pm; May–Aug Tue–Sun 8:30am–5pm; Sept Tue–Sun 8:30am to 4pm; 60 Kč)* and **Valdštejn Castle** *(open Mar, Apr & Oct Sat, Sun and holidays 9am–5pm; May–Sept daily 9am–5:30pm; 40 Kč; www.hrad-valdstejn.cz)*.

Karlovy Vary

113km/70mi west of Prague. Buses depart twice an hour from Prague's Florenc station, approx. 2hrs one way; less frequent trains depart from Prague's main train station, approx. 3hrs one way.

This sleepy spa town is worth visiting both for its colonnaded

Touring Tip

The **Český Krumlov Card**, which costs 200 Kč and is valid for 30 days, is the best deal for exploring the castle. You can purchase a card at the castle.

One Night in Paradise

If you're visiting **Czech Paradise** *(see p 101)* for a weekend, consider starting in Jičín and hiking through the rocks past the **Prachovske skaly** formations. Stop halfway to spend a night at the **Hotel Zámek Hrubá Skála** *(Hrubá Skála 1; 481 659 111; www.hrubaskala.cz)*, a dramatic chateau built into the rock ledge. The next day, complete the route past the Hrubá Skála rocks to finish at Turnov for the return trip to Prague.

promenade, which comes alive each year in early July for the **Karlovy Vary International Film Festival** *(www.kviff.com; see Calendar of Events)*, and for the therapeutic properties of its mineral springs. The shady promenade follows a meandering stream through the west Bohemian valley in which the town sits. Also known as Carlsbad in German, this town was founded in the 14C by King Charles IV, after his hunting party stumbled across the natural springs here. Walking along the promenade, you can pick up a special porcelain cup for sipping the spring water. A fountain for each mineral spring can be found among the colonnades; note that the thermal waters get progressively warmer the farther down the street you go.

Take the funicular behind the Grand Hotel Pupp to the **viewing tower** for vistas over the town. Also be sure to pick up some of the famous *oplátky*, or "spa wafers," that originated in Karlovy Vary and are sold in decorative boxes.

Karlštejn Castle

20km/12.5mi west of Prague in Karlštejn. Trains depart hourly from Prague's main train station, approx. 1hr one way. Open Jun &Sept 9am–6pm, closed Mon; Jul–Aug daily 9am–7pm. Tours cost 100–300 Kč and can be booked online. 311 681 617. www.hradkarlstejn.cz.

One of the easiest places to reach from Prague, popular Karlštejn

Karlštejn Castle

©Michal Boubin/iStockphoto

Castle is pure fairy-tale grandeur. The Gothic castle, founded in 1348, once housed the Bohemian crown jewels. It sits atop a winding series of lanes (packed with kitschy souvenir stands), presiding over the Berounka River below. Extensive reconstruction work has left the castle looking as pristine and imposing as it was centuries ago. Stretch your legs with the 7km/4.5mi hike through the hilly forests to the hamlet of **Svatý Jan pod Skalou**, hailed as the prettiest village in the country.

Konopiště Castle

©Egmont Strigl/age fotostock

Konopiště Castle

40km/25mi south of Prague in Benešov-Konopiště. Buses depart from Prague's Roztyly bus station, approx. 1 hr. Open Tue–Sun Apr, May & Sept 10am–noon and 1pm–4pm, closed Mon; Jun–Aug 10am– noon and 1pm–5pm. Closed Dec–Jan. 30 Kč. 317 721 366. www.zamek-konopiste.cz.

One of the most interesting castles in the region, Konopiště was the home of Archduke Franz Ferdinand d'Este, the successor to the Habsburg throne whose assassination in 1914 triggered the start of World War I. Originally built as a Gothic fortress for the nearby town of Benešov, the 14C French-style Konopiště Castle was remodeled into a residence in the 18C. Nowadays, visitors can tour the Archduke's living quarters, which were restored in the early 1990s. The extensive collection of antlers on the walls testify to d'Este's passion for hunting. In the adjacent **Museum of St. George**, you'll find a vast collection of statues dedicated to the legend of St. George and the dragon. Leave

time to wander in the castle's immaculately maintained English gardens, which make an ideal spot for a picnic.

Křivoklát Castle

58km/36mi west of Prague in Křivoklát. Trains depart every two hours from Prague's main train station, approx. 2 hours (via Beroun). Open May–Sept Tue–Sun 9am–6pm; closed Mon. Hours vary seasonally; check online. www.krivoklat.cz.

Another stately fortress squirreled away in the forested expanses of Central Bohemia, Křivoklát is one of the oldest castles in the Czech lands, dating back to the 12C. In addition to touring the chambers, you can visit a torture museum and take in the view of the surrounding countryside from the Huderka tower. It makes for a leisurely walk of about 12km/7.5mi to follow the winding Rakovnický Stream, leading to the town of Rakovník, which offers bus connections back to Prague.

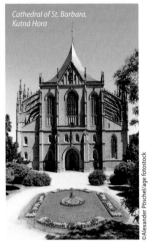
Cathedral of St. Barbara, Kutná Hora

©Alexander Pöschel/age fotostock

an early precursor to the dollar. You can even don a hard hat and descend into the silver mines – not a trip for the claustrophobic. Elsewhere in town, the **Cathedral of St. Barbara** *(Jakubská 1)* is a Gothic wonder of spires, and the **Museum of Alchemy** *(U Jelena 489)* explores the history of man's attempt to unlock the properties of gold.

Lake Lipno

161km/100mi south of Prague in Lipno nad Vltavou. Several buses depart daily from Prague's Florenc station; approx. 6hrs (via Český Krumlov).

This manmade lake, the biggest body of water in the country and the source of the Vltava River, is a veritable seaside in such a landlocked place. It stretches out for 17km/27mi, with sandy beaches and cottage communities set against the sloping pine trees. The town of **Lipno nad Vltavou**, where the dam is based, is a popular base for watersports in the summer (water-skiing, sailing, windsurfing) and skiing in the winter *(check online at www.lipno servis.cz for information about rentals and fees).*

The nearby town of **Frymburk** is a great place to set up camp (literally or figuratively). Stroll its quaint main street, where you'll

Kutná Hora

80.5km/50mi east of Prague. Trains depart every 2hrs from Prague's main station, approx. 1hr one way. Check online for hours and fees for the town's sights: www.kutnahora.cz.

This former silver-mining town has a lot to offer for a day trip, with its morbidly fascinating ossuary, or **bone church** *(Zámecká 127, Kutná Hora-Sedlec)*, a crypt where the remains of 40,000 plague victims are formed into eerie sculptures. The **Czech Museum of Silver** *(Barborská 28)* details the history of mining in the area and the town's invention of the "tolar,"

Eat Like a King

Once you've worked up an appetite walking around **Křivoklát Castle** *(see p 103)*, tuck into succulent game specialties at the **U Jelena** restaurant *(Hradní 53; 313 538 529; www.ujelena.eu)*, decorated in honor of the hunt. The lovely terrace provides good views of the castle and the village's main thoroughfare. U Jelena also has a small bed-and-breakfast upstairs, should you choose to stay for the evening.

find several small hotels with easy access to the beach and the wooded trails. Take the ferry across the river to hike from **Frydava** along the 12km/7.5mi trail up to **Vítkův hrádek**, the ruins of a fortress atop the hill. This vantage point provides sweeping views of the entire lake, and, facing the other way, a panorama of the Austrian Alps.

Litoměřice

55km/34mi north of Prague. Several buses depart daily from Prague's Holešovice station; approx. 1hr one way; several trains depart daily from Holešovice; approx 1.5hrs one way (via Lovosice).

This unique cathedral town, which long ago earned the nickname as "the Garden of Bohemia" due to the lush lowlands that embrace it, can be conveniently combined with a trip to the Terezín Memorial *(see p109)*, just 3km/1.8 away. Litoměřice, with its picturesque town center, makes a good day trip. Be sure to include a visit to the **City Museum** in Old Town Hall, the intricately designed 16C **Black Eagle House**, the spooky town **catacombs**, and the **House at the Chalice**, a Hussite architectural monument *(for information about locations, opening hours and admission fees, check online at: www.litomerice-info.cz).*

Loket

140km/87mi west of Prague. Several buses depart daily from Prague's Florenc station; approx. 2.5hrs one way.

Easily combined with a trip to **Karlovy Vary** just a 20-minute

Dining out in Kutná Hora

If you need to warm your bones after descending into Kutná Hora's silver mines, head to **Dačický** restaurant, a few steps from the main square *(Rakova 8; 327 512 248; www.dacicky.com).* This "old Bohemian tavern," with its sprawling shady beer garden and veritable banquet halls of long wooden tables, is perfect for large groups. Feast on medieval portions of pork knuckle and wild boar goulash, washed down with the local Dačický lager.

Touring Tip

For a bit of adventure and incredible scenery, rent canoes in **Loket** *(two-person canoe 290 Kč; www.putzer.cz)* and paddle down the Ohře 17km/10.5mi to **Karlovy Vary**. The leisurely trip takes about four hours with a stop for lunch.

bus ride away, this tiny town nestled at the elbow *(loket* in Czech) of the Ohře River sees refreshingly few crowds despite its Hollywood-movie history (the main square doubled for Montenegro in the 2006 film *Casino Royale).*
Loket Castle *(open daily Nov–Mar 9am–3:30pm, Apr–Oct 9am–4:30pm; text 80 Kč, guided tour 90 Kč; 352 684 104; www.hradloket.cz)* is rare in that it was never divided into residences like so many other castles. The town also has a microbrewery, St. Florian, which has a pleasant patio overlooking the river.

Town Hall Wine Cellar

For a memorable meal on the main square of **Litoměřice** *(see p 105)*, duck your head at the low doorway and enter the **Radniční sklípek** *(Mírové náměstí 21/13; 416 731 142; www.radnicni-sklipek.cz)*, a romantic brick-lined cellar serving up amazing lamb and pork entrées by candlelight.

♨ Mariánské lázně

166km/103mi west of Prague. Several trains depart daily from Prague's main station; approx. 3hrs one way.

Also known as Marienbad in German, Mariánské lázně is a spa town in West Bohemia, quieter and more remote than its more famous neighbor, Karlovy Vary. Don't expect wild nightlife or much activity. The natural beauty speaks for itself, and there's a prescription for relaxation that most people follow: a visit to the local therapeutic spas and a peaceful walk into the hilly countryside dominated by the Slavkov Forest.

Mělník

35km/24mi north of Prague. Buses depart twice hourly from either Prague's Florenc or Holešovice stations; approx. 1 hr.

This Bohemian town, a regional capital and a wine-producing twin to the Hungarian town of Tokaj, has more in common with its South Moravian wine brethren than with the flatlands of Bohemia. Rising up through hillside vineyards at the confluence of the Elbe (Labe) and Vltava rivers, **Mělník Chateau** *(Zámecká 1; open year-round daily 10am–6pm; 90 Kč; 315 622 121)* is a bastion of the town. From its grounds, views stretch over the region, and in the courtyard, the **Zámek cukárna** sweetshop has luscious cakes to enjoy with a cup of coffee. Check out the pretty main square with its colorful Renaissance houses, learn about the history of the region and local wine making at the **Regional Museum Mělník** on the square *(open Tue–Sun 9am–noon and 1pm–5pm; 315 630 936; www.muzeum-melnik.cz)*, perhaps stopping to sample the local St. Ludmila wines at the museum's

Mělník

©Gilles Barbier/age fotostock

café. Then take a trip down into the eerie catacombs below the town. Several kilometers to the east is **Kokořínsko National Park** *(www.sdruzenikokorinsko.cz).*

Mikulov

248km/154mi southeast of Prague. Several trains depart daily from Prague's main station; approx. 4.5hrs (via Brno or Břeclav).

In the eastern part of the Czech Republic, close to the border with Austria, this town sits in the heart of Moravian wine country and feels more like Italy than Central Europe – indeed, it was designed by Italian architects. Renaissance buildings and terraces overflowing with flowers make a colorful backdrop for the swaths of vineyards that stretch for miles. Mikulov, set on a hill overlooking the vineyards, hosts regular wine festivals throughout the spring and summer *(check for event information at www.mikulov.cz).* A network of wine towns and villages here are connected by cycling trails.

Okoř Castle

14km/9mi north of Prague. Open Jun–Sept Tue–Sun, closed Mon; Oct– Dec and Apr–May 10am–4pm. 5 –75 Kč. 233 900 675. www.hrad-okor.cz. Buses depart every two hours from Dejvická, approx. 40min.

The ruins of this fortress are within easy reach of Prague, and the surrounding area is perfect for an afternoon stroll. The castle, which dates to the 13C, went through periods of Gothic and Renaissance incarnations, before being severely damaged in the Thirty Years' War; after that it was reconstructed in

Mikulov Castle, Mikulov

©Henryk T Kaiser/age fotostock

the Baroque style. The ruins here serve as a perfect setting for one of the region's medieval fairs in summer, perhaps the best time to visit *(www.festivalokor.cz).*

Orlík

68km/42mi south of Prague. Several buses depart daily from Prague's Na Knížecí station, approx. 1.5 hrs.

The castle in this town is just one of the many attractions in this area of South Bohemia. There's also a manmade lake, and the area has gained a reputation as a vacation destination, popular with windsurfers and hikers. **Orlík Castle** *(open Jun–Aug 9am–6pm, rest of the year hours vary; 90 Kč; 382 275 101; www.schwarzenberg. cz)* cuts an imposing silhouette against the lake. Built as a royal castle in the 13C, the façade is a brilliant white, with classic round turrets in the Romantic Gothic style. The castle is within walking distance of the area's largest village, **Orlík nad Vltavou**, location of myriad watersports concessions, vacation rentals and restaurants.

Pubs in Pilsen

Beer tastes best straight from the source, and fans of **Pilsner Urquell** will surely work up a thirst touring the brewery. A good bet for fresh, unpasteurized pints of Pilsner is **Na Parkánu**, a cozy pub attached to the Brewery Museum and decked out in wood and copper accents with a nice garden (*Veleslavínova 4; 377 324 485; www.naparkanu.cz*). Or expand your palate at **Klub malých pivovarů** (*Nádraží 16; 774 790 979; www.klubmalychpivovaru.cz*), which serves several types of regional microbrews.

Pilsen
(Plzeň)

90km/56mi west of Prague. Buses depart regularly from Prague's Zličín station; approx. 1hr; hourly trains from the main station take approx. 1hr 50min.

A visit to this West Bohemian regional capital is a must for any beer lover; Pilsen is a true mecca for fans of the light, pilsner style of lager that takes its name from this town. In addition to touring the **Pilsner Urquell Brewery**, the city has an interesting **Old Town** and a buzzing student vibe (Pilsen is home to several universities). Take in history at the **Great Synagogue** (*Sady Pětatřicátníků 35/11*), brush up on your puppetry skills at the **Puppet Museum** (*Náměstí Republiky 23; open Tue–Sun 10am–6pm; 60 Kč ; 378 370 801; www.muzeumloutek.cz*), or visit the **Patton Memorial** (*KD Peklo, Pobřežní 10; open Tue–Sun 9am–1pm & 2pm–5pm; 60 Kč ; 377 320 414; www.pattonmemorial.cz*), which commemorates the liberation of the city by US troops in May 1945.

The Pilsner Urquell line also includes the lighter Gambrinus lager, as well as the Kozel lager, both light and dark (the dark lager is especially rich). More recently, Pilsner added the Master brand – a strong dark lager – to its lineup.

Průhonice

14.5km/9mi south of Prague. Buses depart regularly from Metro C station Opatov; approx. 15 min.

So close to Prague that it's considered a suburb, the village of Průhonice has become a desired location just south of the city. A visit to **Průhonice Chateau** (*Květnové náměstí 1; open daily May–Sept 7am–8pm, rest of the year hours vary; 40 Kč; 267 750 346*) and its tranquil path-laced gardens makes this town worth a detour. Průhonice is also home to the family-centered **Aquapalace** waterpark (*Prazska 138; open daily 10am-10pm; prices vary; 271 104 111; www.aquapalace.cz*).

🏔 Šumava National Park

Approx. 137km/85mi south of Prague. Several trains depart daily for Železná Ruda from Prague's main station; approx. 4 hrs.

A veritable wonderland of forests and hills, this 680km^2/263sq mi national park in South Bohemia provides ample opportunities for hiking and cycling in warmer months and skiing in winter.

Průhonice

©Tom Parizek/iStockphoto

Peaceful villages are dotted with wooden houses – the village of **Volary**, in particular, is known for its folk architecture. Transportation to the area is a bit tricky by public means, so it's best to rent a car to explore this vast park. The towns of Prachatice, Vimperk and Železná Ruda (from where you can hike to a glacial lake), in particular, are good starting points, and the stunning village of **Kvilda** ranks as one of the loftiest in the country.

Terezín Memorial

64km/40mi north of Prague, in Terezin. Several buses depart daily from Prague's Holešovice station; approx. 1 hr. Hours vary seasonally. Check online at www.pamatnik-terezin.cz.

The town of Terezín was changed forever during World War II, when the Nazis set up what they claimed was a model Jewish ghetto – really a concentration camp and transfer center to infamous places like Auschwitz. Today, the remains of the Magdeburg Barracks and

grounds are a sobering reminder of the past, and the site is being considered as the future home of a European Holocaust Memorial. The touching **Ghetto Museum** *(museum and barracks open daily Apr–Oct 9am–6pm, Nov–Mar 9am–5:30pm; 160 Kč)* takes a reflective look back at the many people who passed through these gates.

The Cottage Tradition

Under the Communist regime, the Czechs were limited in their travel options, to say the least. Starting in the mid-20C, it became popular for every family to own a *chalupa*, or cottage, in the countryside, where people could talk freely, drink around the campfire and tend their gardens. The tradition still continues, and it's not uncommon for locals to vacate Prague on summer weekends. If you have enough time and are looking for a relaxing escape, cottages can be rented inexpensively *(www.interbohemia.cz).*

EXCURSIONS

FAMILY FUN

There's more to Prague than just churches and monuments. From paddling on the Vltava River to finding your way through a mirror maze, Prague has plenty of attractions to appeal to both young visitors and to the child in all of us.

Boat Tour on the Vltava

Dvořákovo nábřeží (embankment) next to St. Agnes' Convent, Old Town. Departs at noon & 4pm. 190 Kč adults; 95 Kč children 3-11. 774 278 473. www.cruise-prague.cz.

To avoid the crowds that flood the cobblestone streets, consider taking a boat tour on the Vltava River to see Prague's sites. One-hour cruises depart twice daily and feature a sundeck on top for soaking up the rays as you gaze out at the sights. Accompanying commentary is available in seven languages.

Funicular to Petřín Hill

Lesser Town (entrance close to tram stop. Trams 12 or 20: Ujezd. Runs Apr–Oct every 10min, Nov–Mar every 15min. 26 Kč (adult transfer tickets), 18 Kč (adult non-transfer tickets). www.dpp.cz.

The funicular running up Petřín Hill in the Lesser Town dates all the way back to 1851, and is a great way to ascend to the park *(see Parks And Gardens)* without huffing and puffing up its winding paths – especially with young children in tow. On the way to the top, the funicular makes two stops, including one for the restaurant **Nebozizek** *(see Must Eat)*. From here it's an easy stroll to the **Petřín Tower**, the **Mirror Maze** or the Rose Gardens.

Horse-drawn Carriage Rides

Pick-up on Old Town Square or by request at hotels. Metro A: Staroměstská. 1–4 people 2,700 Kč; with guide, additional 600 Kč/hr. 773 103 102. www.private-prague-guide.com.

Experience the charm of Prague as it was through the ages – by horse-drawn carriage. One-hour tours meander through Old Town, passing the quarter's most historic sites. Seeing the sights from a plush carriage straight out of *Cinderella* is sure to charm both young and old.

Take a Paddleboat

Slovansky Island, New Town. Trams 6, 9, 17 or 18: Národní třída. Open daily Apr–Oct 11am–11pm. Paddle boats 150 Kč per hour; illuminated boats (8pm–11pm) 200 Kč per hour. 777 800 003. If you'd rather navigate the river under your own power, rent a paddle boat on the Vltava River. Based on Slovansky Island in New Town, just next to the National Theater, the boats give you good perspectives on Old Town and Lesser Town. The swan-shaped paddle boats are sure to delight the kids.

Mirror Maze
©Prague Information Service

Lego Museum

Národní 31, New Town. Metro B: Národní třída. Open year-round daily 10am–8pm. 200 Kč adults; 130 Kč children. 775 446 677. www.muzeumlega.cz.

Prague's Lego Museum claims to be the biggest in Europe, and it certainly is a fun way to spend an afternoon indoors. With more than 2,000 models on display, and 20 themed exhibits, the museum is a true homage to the timeless building blocks. There's also a play area where kids can create their own Lego masterpieces.

Mirror Maze
(Bludiště)

In Petřín Park, Petřínské sady, Lesser Town. Tram 12 or 20: Ujezd. Open May–Aug daily 10am–8pm, Apr & Sept daily 10am–7pm (Oct until 6pm), Jan–Mar Sat–Sun 10am–5pm. 70 Kč adults; 50 Kč children ages 6-15; 20 Kč children under 6. 724 911 497. www. petrinska-rozhledna.cz.

Petřín Hill is home to many wonders, one of which is the Mirror Maze. From the outside, it's a fairy-tale fortress of a 19C building; inside is a maze of mirrors sure to distort your perception of reality and make you laugh at your reflection. Walking through the maze takes about half an hour – that is, if you can find your way out!

Petřín Tower
(Petřínská rozhledna)

On Petřín Hill, Petřínské sady, Lesser Town. Tram 12 or 20: Ujezd; then walk or take the funicular railway. Open daily Apr–Sept 10am–10pm, Oct & Mar 10am–8pm, Nov–Feb 10am–6pm. 100 Kč adults; 50 Kč children ages 6-15; 20 Kč children under 6. 724 911 497. www.petrinska-rozhledna.cz.

One of the city's unique sites is Prague's Eiffel Tower, a scaled-down version built for the 1891 Jubilee Exhibition. Its perch atop Petřín Hill gives it an unbeatable lookout over the entire city, and its magnificent wooden and metal structure rises 60m/197ft high; on a blustery day, you can feel it swaying slightly as it gives in the wind, as it was designed to do. Climbing the 299 steps to the top makes for some breathtaking – literally – views.

Planetarium

Královská obora 233, in Stromovka Park, Holešovice. Open year-round Mon & Sun 8:30am–noon & 1pm–6pm, Tue–Thu & Sat 8:30am–noon & 1pm–8pm. Closed Fri. 220 999 001. www.planetarium.cz.

In the middle of a lush park, the Planetarium offers a varied program of shows for English speakers, including one on celestial bodies, and one on alchemy in the court of Rudolf II in the 1600s. English-language headphones are available for any of the Czech programs.

Prague Zoo

U Trojského zámku 3, Troja. Metro C: Holešovice, or bus 112 to Zoologicka zakrada. Open Jun–Aug 9am–7pm, Apr–May & Sept–Oct 9am–6pm. Rest of the year, hours vary. 150 Kč adults; 100 Kč children ages 3-15, children under 3 free. 296 112 111. www.zoopraha.cz.

It's worth dedicating a day to the Prague Zoo, as its vast network of paths and exhibits makes for a lovely stroll, as well as a fun look at the animals. Opened to the public in 1931, the zoo was damaged severely in the devastating floods of August 2002, when more than half of the property and animals were lost. However, an extensive reconstruction campaign has resulted in the zoo being even more impressive than before. A **petting zoo** delights curious little ones, while a **chairlift** takes you up the hill and affords sweeping views over Prague. State-of-the-art exhibits include the **Indonesian Jungle**, where you can walk among misty trees and ponds and observe monkeys, birds and other critters. Check the zoo's website for feeding schedules.

A Boat to the Zoo

224 931 013 or 017. For schedules, check online at paroplavba.cz. Even the trip to the zoo can be an adventure. A special boat runs regularly from Rašínovo Quay near Palacky Square to the zoo, a journey lasting about 75 minutes. Youngsters can enjoy the adventure of cruising on the river, while adults can enjoy a glass of wine at the onboard bar.

Sea World
(Morsky svet)

At Výstaviště in Holešovice. Tram 17: Výstaviště. Open year-round daily 10am–7pm. 280 Kč adults; 180 Kč children under 15 (free for children under 1m/3ft tall). 220 103 275. www.morsky-svet.cz.

Despite the fact that the Czech Republic is a landlocked country, it's still possible to see exotic fish and other denizens of the deep in Prague at Sea World, the largest aquarium in the country. Elaborate coral reefs have been re-created here to house hundreds of species of fish and sea creatures, including 3m/10ft-long sharks, lion fish from the Indian Ocean, and predatory barracudas from the Atlantic. Check at admission desk for animal feeding schedules.

MUST DO

A 19th-century Treat

The streets of Prague are crisscrossed with tram lines, and public transport has long been a popular way for city dwellers to get around. Starting in 1875, a system of tram lines was formed, with cars originally pulled by horses. In 1891, the first electric car was unveiled, leading the way for the routes to easily connect suburbs with the city center. Today, hopping on and off the trams can be a fun way to design your own itinerary to explore Prague's residential areas.

Take a Tram Ride

Tram runs Mar–Nov Sat–Sun; check website for exact times. 35 Kč adults; 20 Kč children under 15. 296 124 902. www.dpp.cz.

Take a journey through the city on **Tram Line 91** aboard one of the historic red-and-white trams that are decked out with wooden benches. Trams run regularly on weekends (except in winter) and start at the Střešovice depot *(at Patočkova and Cukrovarnická Sts., in Střešovice)*, calling at stops near Prague Castle, Lesser Town Square, Národní třída (National Avenue), Wenceslas Square, and other popular sightseeing spots.

Toy Museum

©Yadid Levy/age fotostock

Toy Museum
(Muzeum hracek)

*Jiřská 4, **Hradčany**. Tram 22: Pražský hrad. Open year-round daily 9:30am–5:30pm. 60 Kč adults; 30 Kč children; 120 Kč family. 224 372 294.*

The whole family will enjoy the Toy Museum, which is located within the grounds of Prague Castle and bills itself as the second-largest in the world. Seven exhibition rooms present the history of toys with examples from all over the world dating back to ancient Greece. Little girls will love the large Barbie collection, while boys will gravitate toward the toy trains.

Take a tram ride

©Sylvain Grandadam/age fotostock

THE GREAT OUTDOORS

Czechs are great lovers of the outdoors, be it hiking or biking or merely enjoying a beer in the sun at one of Prague's many beer gardens. And their love for team sports is likewise notable – especially soccer and ice-hockey, two sports in which the country has scored big wins in international competitions. If you want to stretch your legs and get some exercise, take a run, a walk or a bike ride through some of Prague's numerous parks and get a feel for nature within the city limits.

🚲 Bicycling

Several companies specialize in bike rentals and offer bike tours of the city. One is **City Bike Prague** (*Královdvorská 5, Old Town; 776 180 284; open Apr–Oct daily 9am–7pm; Metro A: Staroměstská; 2hr rental 300 Kč, all-day rental 500 Kč; www.citybike-praguecom*), which offers a variety of tours and rentals. Another option is **Praha Bike** (*Dlouhá 24, Old Town; 732 388 880, open daily 9am–8pm; Metro B: Náměstí Republiky; www.prahabike.cz*). In addition to regular rentals (*200 Kč for 2hrs; 590 Kč for 24hrs*), Praha Bike features organized trips into the surrounding countryside, such as a day ride to **Karlštejn Castle** (*see Excursions*).

🥾 Hiking in Prague

Tram 26 or 20: Divoká Šárka.

While there are countless parks and nature preserves to explore in Prague, one of the best is **Divoká Šárka**, a vast, wild expanse on the city limits (*30min from Wenceslas Square*) where trails lead you through hilly forests and past dramatic cliffs. It's best to arm yourself with a map (like the Czech Tourist Club map for Praha-zapad, available at most Prague bookshops) to keep track of the paths. On sunny weekends, Wild Šárka (as the name translates in English) becomes a veritable promenade of dog-walkers and families with strollers, but the park is big enough that you will still

Žluté lázně

©Žluté lázně

Beware of Ticks!

If you're planning to head out by foot or bike into grassy areas, make sure to spray yourself with a heavy-duty bug spray that specifically repels ticks. Deer ticks are very prevalent in this area of Central Europe, and are known to inhabit any area of tall grass, even within the city. Ticks here can carry both Lyme disease and the serious tick-borne encephalitis. Make sure to keep your feet and ankles covered for added protection, and, stock up on special anti-tick sprays at any Prague *lékárna* (pharmacy).

find a sense of tranquility. Divoká Šárka also features a stream-fed outdoor swimming pool, nestled into the cliffs.

Žluté lázně

Podolské nábřeží 3, Podoli. Trams 3, 16, 17 or 21: Dvorce. Open in summer 9am–2am. 80 Kč from 9am–5pm; free after 5pm. 244 463 777. www.zlutelazne.cz.

The closest thing to a beach in Prague, this outdoor riverfront complex has the feel and the fun of a cheesy Ibiza-style resort. Sandy "beaches" come complete with bamboo cabanas, table-tennis, pétanque, beach volleyball and countless walk-up beach bars that turn into dance clubs come nightfall. A children's play area will keep the young ones entertained.

SPECTATOR SPORTS

Ice Hockey

Ice hockey is by far the most popular local pastime, both playing it and watching it. The Czech professional league, the **O2 Extraliga**, has an outstanding international reputation, and many of its players go on to join NHL teams in the US and Canada. The season runs from mid-September through April, and the biggest

ice-hockey venue in Prague is the **Tesla Arena** *(Za Elektrárnou 419, Holešovice; 266 727 443; www. hcsparta.cz)*.

Get tickets for upcoming games online at *www.ticketportal.cz*, or through the arena's box office. **Sazka Arena** *(Ocelářská 460, Vysocany; 266 121 122; www.hc-slavia.cz)*, also hosts big games, as well as rock concerts and other large-scale events.

Soccer

Czechs have long had a love affair with the Great Game, and for a true local experience – especially if you're a soccer fan – it's worth going to a match of the Czech **Gambrinus liga**. The league is made up of 16 clubs, and the season runs from August to May, with teams playing 30 games each. Noted Prague teams include Sparta Prague, Bohemians 1905 and Slavia Prague. Games are usually played on weekends, and regular venues include the **Sparta Stadium** *(Milady Horákové 98, Letna; 296 111 400; www.sparta.cz)*, where tickets range from 100 Kč to 400 Kč (more, if it's a big international game). Big games sell out quickly; for many lower-tier games, you can buy tickets on match day.

BOX OFFICE

PERFORMING ARTS

From its rich marionette tradition to hosting the world premier of Mozart's *Don Giovanni*, Prague has long been a spectacular scene for the performing arts. Many of the city's venues have stories as fantastic as those portrayed on the stage, and a wealth of underground jazz bars provide the perfect way to mellow out in the evening *(see Nightlife)*. The uninitiated will be enchanted by black-light theater, one of Prague's most celebrated genres, while the gilded Baroque interiors of the **National Theater★★★** or the **State Opera** will have opera fans swooning in their seats.

National Theater★★★
(Národní divadlo)

Ostrovní 1, New Town. Trams 6, 9, 18 or 22: Národní divadlo. 224 901 638. www.narodni-divadlo.cz.

A landmark in Prague by its own right, the National Theater has come to symbolize the Czech nation. Funded through a nationwide collection, the theater was completed in 1881 and destroyed by fire two weeks later. Work on the new theater was led by **Josef Schultz**, who rebuilt it in the Renaissance Revival style. The sculptor **Josef Myslbek** created the statues that decorate the façade on the Vltava side. If you attend a performance, note the curtain decoration depicting the contribution of the Czech people to the building's funding. From the outside, make sure to look up at the roof, which is visible from down the river with its brilliant gold and blue hues. In addition to being an iconic structure, the National is also the top theater in the country, staging opera, drama and ballet, with performances both here in its beautiful halls as well as at other theaters around the city. Between 1977 and 1983, the National Theater was enlarged on the eastern side with the addition of the **Nová scéna**, whose glass-brick façade has been compared to bubble wrap.

National Theater

MUST DO

Lucerna Palace★★
(Palác Lucerna)

Vodičkova 36, New Town.
Metro A or B: Můstek. 224 217 108.
www.lucerna.cz.

This sprawling complex of shops, restaurants, pubs and music venues takes up about two blocks just off of Wenceslas Square. Inside, the **Lucerna Music Bar** *(www.musicbar.cz)* hosts regular concerts of international pop, rock and jazz acts as well as weekly themed discos, while the **Lucerna Grand Hall**, a tiered ballroom from yesteryear, stages larger classical acts and sell-out shows.

Estates Theater★
(Stavovské divadlo)

Ovocny trh 6, Old Town.
Metro A or B: Můstek.
www.narodni-divadlo.cz.

Part of the National Theater, this grand house located between Wenceslas Square and Old Town Square is worth a visit for its grand interiors alone, not to mention its program of opera, musicals and ballet. Mozart first premiered his opera *Don Giovanni* here in 1787, putting Prague on the performing-arts map for good.

⚜ Rudolfinum★

Alšovo nábřeží 79/12, Josefov.
Metro A: Staroměstská.
www.ceskafilharmonie.cz.

Named in honor of Crown Prince Rudolf of Hapsburg, this 1884 Renaissance Revival beauty is the home of the **Czech Philharmonic Orchestra**. The 1,200-seat **Rudolfinum★** *(see Historic Sites)*, the largest concert hall in

Café Slavia
Smetanovo nábřeží 2, Old Town. Trams 6, 9, 18 or 22: Národní divadlo. 224 239 604. www.cafeslavia.cz. A Prague legend and a great spot to grab a cup of coffee or a cocktail after the theater, Café Slavia shines for its historic setting lined by gilded walls as well as for its fine coffees and mixed drinks. Try to score a table with a river view. Nightly after 7pm, live piano music pumps up the class factor.

Prague, also hosts visiting musical luminaries from the classical and jazz spheres. Attending a performance here is a special treat.

Akropolis Palace
(Palác Akropolis)

Kubelíkova 27, Žižkov. 296 330 911. www.palacakropolis.cz.

There's always something of interest going on at Akropolis, the hippest venue in town. From international rock bands to local theater and performance art, every artist aspires to play this unique and lively venue in Prague. Located in the über-cool residential area of Žižkov, Akropolis also has several bars, a café, and a restaurant that's open late.

Hybernia Theatre

Náměstí Republiky 4, Old Town.
Metro B: Náměstí Republiky. 211 141 600. www.hybernia.eu.

Recently reopened to the public after an extensive facelift, the Hybernia Theatre may pale in comparison with the **Municipal House★★★** *(see Architectural*

PERFORMING ARTS

Landmarks), which it faces, but it has a charm and a repertoire all its own. The building predates its more famous neighbor, having been built before Charles IV founded New Town. Originally a monastery and later a church, the structure was converted into a theater in 2006. It now hosts hit musicals and more.

Image Black Light Theatre

Pařížská 4, Josefov. 222 329 191.
Metro A: Staroměstská.
www.imagetheatre.cz.

Truly a remarkable experience, black-light theater originated in Asia, but has become a specialty of Prague. Seated in a completely darkened room in a black-box theater, you will see stories unfold before you in the shapes of dancing creatures and actors in fluorescent costumes illuminated by black light.

Jazz Boat

Gate No. 5, Dvořákovo nábřeží, under the Čechův Bridge, Josefov.
Tram 17: Pravnicke fakulta.
731 183 180. www.jazzboat.cz.

Yearning to see the sights of Prague while listening to the latest top-notch jazz concert? The Jazz Boat combines both, with nightly summer cruises up and down the Vltava, passing **Prague Castle★★★**, **Charles Bridge★★★** and the **National Theater★★★**.

Malostranská beseda

Malostranske náměstí 21, Lesser Town. Trams 12, 20 or 22: Malostranske náměstí.
www.malostranska-beseda.cz.

One of the arcaded Renaissance buildings on **Lesser Town Square★** *(see Historic Squares)*, this complex has it all: a restaurant, a café, a gallery and several performance spaces, with regular offerings of local folk and jazz music as well as small theater troupes. The building, which has served as a cultural center for more than 100 years, reopened in 2010 after extensive renovations.

National Marionette Theatre

Žatecká 1, Old Town. Metro A: Staroměstská. 224 819 322.
www.mozart.cz.

Křižík's Fountain (Křižíkova Fontana)

In the Výstaviště Praha complex, U Výstaviště 1/20, Holešovice. Trams 5, 12 or 15: Výstaviště. 200 Kč. 723 665 694. www.krizikovafontana.cz.
Not to be confused with the demure **Singing Fountain** *(see Palaces)*, this fountain is a blast for the whole family. It was built as an electrically lit water feature for the 1891 World Exposition and has been updated since then with 1,300 multicolored reflectors, 3,000 nozzles and 49 water pumps. Paired with well-known soundtracks and music by famous composers, the spectacle springs to life nightly on the hour between 8pm and 11pm *(10pm on Sun; see website for details)*, with dancers and actors adding to the show.

For the child inside everyone enthralled with puppetry, a visit to the National Marionette Theatre is a must. The troupe's vibrant version of *Don Giovanni*, performed in the Art Decor Municipal Library, is particularly enchanting.

New Stage
(Nová scena)

Národní 4, New Town. Metro B: Národní třída. 224 931 482. www.novascena.cz.

A striking contrast exists between the modern, jutted angles of the Rubic's Cube-like New Stage (1983) and the historic National Theater headquarters next door. Part of the **National Theater★★★**, the New Stage hosts the famed theater troupe Laterna magika, as well as performances of

New Stage

contemporary and experimental dance and theater.

State Opera
(Státní Opera Praha)

Legerova 75, New Town. Metro A or C: Muzeum. 296 117 111. www.opera.cz.

Any opera buff will want to make a beeline for the National Theater's State Opera, located between the National Museum and the main train station in New Town. Opened as the Prague German Stage in 1888, the State Opera has a breathtaking auditorium, with intricate Rococo designs and gleaming gold accents. The regular program includes both classic operas and modern ballet.

Švandovo Theater
(Švandovo divadlo)

Štefánikova 57, Smíchov. Metro B: Smíchov. 234 651 111. www.svandovodivadlo.cz.

This cutting-edge modern theater performs all of its shows with simultaneous English subtitles, making Czech-language theater – which boasts both a rich and varied history and a thriving, innovative present – accessible to visitors.

PERFORMING ARTS

SHOPPING

Shops are everywhere in Prague, and in-between the T-shirts and Russian nesting dolls, you can hone in on some high-quality local crafts. You'll notice the sparkling Bohemian crystal first, but you'll also see wooden toys, garnet and amber jewelry, and ceramics. If it's fashion you're after, check out the blossoming scene of young local designers.

SHOPPING STREETS

The areas most crammed with souvenir and crafts shops include **Mostecká**, **Nerudova★★** and U Lužického semináře in Lesser Town; and Celetná, Melantrichova and Kaprova in Old Town. For straight-up retail, **Wenceslas Square★★★** and **Na Příkopě★★** harbor many respected international chains.

🛍 Pařížská třída★★ (Paris Street)

Josefov. Metro A: Staroměstská.

Built at the turn of the 20C to resemble the Champs Elysée in Paris, Pařížská is Prague's most chi-chi shopping area. The leafy boulevard, which extends from

Old Town Square to the Vltava riverfront, is chock-a-block with top-name designer boutiques (think Prada, Burberry and Hermès). The street bisects the Jewish Town and is within easy reach of many cozy cafes and bars, perfect spots to wind down after a spending spree.

Czech Handicrafts

🛍 Galerie Marionette

*U Lužichého semináře 7, **Lesser Town**. Metro A: Malostranská. Open Mon–Sat 10am–6pm. 257 535 091.*

At this gallery, the marionettes may be more expensive than most other places, but every piece on display is the result of long hours of work by local artisans.

Manufaktura

*Melantrichova 17, **Old Town**. Metro A or B: Můstek. Open Mon–Sat 10am–8pm. 221 632 480. www.manufaktura.cz*

One of the largest satellites in Prague of Manufaktura chain, this place sells wooden toys and handmade soaps, among other handcrafted objects.

Decorative Arts

Art Décoratif

*U Obecního domu, **New Town**. Metro B: Náměstí Republiky. Open daily 10am–8pm. 222 002 350.*

Manufaktura

MUST DO

This gorgeous shop sets the Prague standard for lamps, furniture and jewelry in the Secessionist style.

Artěl Glass
Celetná 29 (enter through Rybná 1), Old Town. Metro B: Náměstí Republiky. Open daily 11am–7pm. www.artelglass.com.
Sparkling crystal and glass objects here reflect traditional expertise and contemporary shapes. Founded in 1988 by American Karen Feldman, Artěl Glass features antiques as well as modern pieces.

Český porcelain
Perlová 1, Old Town. Metro A or B: Můstek. Open Mon–Fri 9am–6pm, Sat 9am–1pm. 224 210 955. www.cesky.porcelan.cz.
Traditional Bohemian porcelain can be identified easily by its "onion"-print design. This shop offers a large selection of products in this style, as well as a range of textiles.

Keramika V Ungeltu
Týn 7, Old Town. Metro B: Náměstí Republiky. Open daily 10am–8pm.
Moms will appreciate the traditional ceramic wares here, which include vessels with the traditional blue and white "onion" design, while the kids will delight in the host of wooden toys of every size.

Material
Týn 1, Old Town. Metro A: Staroměstská. Open daily 10:30am–8pm. 608 664 766. www.i-material.com.
Looking for beautiful hand-blown objects in Bohemian crystal? You'll find lots of them in this little shop in the Ungelt Courtyard.

Moser
Na Příkopě 12, New Town. Metro A or B: Můstek. Open daily 10am–8pm. 224 211 293. www.moser-glass.com.
This factory store features magnificent Bohemian crystal and porcelain pieces from the town of Karlovy Vary, where a factory has been making them since 1857.

Qubus
Rámová 3, Old Town. Metro B: Náměstí Republiky. Open Mon–Fri 10am–6pm. www.qubus.cz.
Drop by this shop, if not to buy, then to admire the witty porcelain creations of Maxim Velcovský.

Umělecké Sklenářství
Umilosrdných 35, Old Town. Metro A: Staroměstská. Open Mon–Fri 8am–5pm. 737 666 851. www.vitraz.cz.
Founded in 1935 by the famous Czech stained-glass artist Josef Jiříčka, the workshop specializes in restoring antiques from a variety of periods.

SHOPPING

U Škopků

*U Lužického semináře 22, **Lesser Town**. Metro A: Malostranská. Open daily 11am–8pm (5pm in winter). 257 531 926.*

Close to Charles Bridge, U Škopků boasts handmade replicas of Gothic, Baroque, Renaissance, Charles IV- and Rudolf II-era glasses at very reasonable prices.

Fashion

Adelaide

*Jungmannova 3, **New Town**. Metro B: Národní třída. Open Mon–Fri 10am–7pm, Sat 10am–5pm. 222 525 279. www.adelaidefashion.cz.*

This talented designer does hand-painted children's clothing, colorful casual clothes and formal wear for women, in addition to accessories and jewelry.

Granát Turnov

*Dlouhá 30, **Old Town**. Metro B: Náměstí Republiky. Open Mon–Fri 10am–6pm, Sat 10am–1pm. 222 315 612. www.granat.cz.*

Find Bohemian garnets – a gem Prague is renowned for – in the form of pendants, rings, bracelets and necklaces here, straight from the Turnov art production cooperative.

Helena Fejková Gallery

*Štěpánská 61, **New Town** (first floor of Lucerna Palace). Metro A or B: Můstek. Open Mon–Fri 10am–7pm, Sat 10am–3pm. 724 125 262. www.helenafejkova.cz.*

One of the great Czech designers, Helena Fejková conceives elegant, understated designs for both men and women. Her store, in the Lucerna passage, will give you a chance to try out one of the rare "paternoster" elevators still in service (the elevator doesn't stop; you have to hop out when you reach your floor).

Ivana Follová Atelier

*Mezibranská 9, **New Town**. Metro A or C: Můzeum. Open Mon–Fri 9am–2pm (or by appointment). 222 211 357. www.ivanafollova.cz.*

Although Ivana Follová's pricey designs are understated, she has no problem mixing materials or coming up with asymmetrical designs. Check out the selection of unusual headpieces.

La Femme Mimi

*Havelská 1, **Old Town**. Metro A or B: Můstek. Open daily 10am–6:30pm. 224 241 389. www.lafemmemimi.cz.*

Using satin, silks, raw cotton and other fabrics imported from Asia, Mimi Lang fashions unique clothing inspired both by Asian traditions and European fashion. Complete your ensemble with the shop's costume jewelry and handbags.

Parazit

*Karlova 25, **Old Town**. Metro A: Staroměstská. Open Mon–Fri 11am–8pm, Sat 11am–7pm. 357 231 428. www.parazit.cz.*

Eva Dudasová Turková and Adriana Hajová intended on breaking with fashion's dictates in opening this shop – and they have remained true to their promise.

Vintage

*Michalská 18, **Old Town**. Metro A: Staroměstská. Open Mon–Fri 11am–7pm, Sat 11am–6pm, Sun noon–5pm. 774 273 238. www.vintage–clothes.cz.*

Fotografic

©Martin Fojtek/Fotografic

Tired of what's in your suitcase? At Vintage, you'll find a range of designs – from fancy to informal – dating from decades past, as well as vintage-inspired items by current designers.

Books and Photography

Fotografic
*Stříbrná 2, **Old Town**. Trams 17 or 18: Karlovy lázně. Open daily 1pm–7pm. www.fotografic.cz.*
Beautiful photos and prints of Prague – and elsewhere – abound here, available in several formats and printed on canvas.

Knihkupectví Klub Architektů
*Betlémské náměstí, **Old Town**. Metro B: Národní třída. Open Mon–Sat 10am–8pm, Sun noon–8pm.*

Located in the courtyard next to the Bethlehem Chapel, the Architects Club bookstore carries a large variety of architecture books, with a particular focus on Prague. You'll also find good books on Cubism and Functionalism in the Czech Republic.

Wine

Vinograf
*Míšeňská 8, **Lesser Town**. Metro A: Malostranská. Open Mon–Fri 1pm–midnight, Sat–Sun 3pm–1am. 604 705 730. www.vinograf.cz.*
A great address if you want to taste Czech or Slovak wines, this little cellar in the Lesser Town offers a range of prices for every budget. Join the regulars for a drink here, if you can manage to snag a seat.

🏛 Palladium
If you're looking for one-stop-shopping and international chains, head to the **Palladium mall**, on Republic Square *(open Mon–Sat 9am–10pm, Sun until 9pm; www.palladiumpraha.cz)*. You can't miss it: The converted former monastery building looks like a pink wedding cake. Inside you'll find clothing, sports equipment, cosmetics, shoes, books and more under one roof. In December, the mall's front windows become a luminous Advent calendar display.

NIGHTLIFE

The Czechs have a well-earned reputation as the world's biggest beer drinkers, and you never have to walk farther than half a block before seeing a welcoming sign beckoning you into a centuries-old pub or beer hall. The city comes alive after dark – and while Prague doesn't have a specific nightlife district, there are many places where you can easily dance until dawn. (Cover charges may apply.)

Bars and Pubs

Fraktal
Šmeralova 1, Bubeneč. Trams 1, 8, 15, 25 or 26: Letenské náměstí. 777 794 094. www.fraktalbar.cz.
This sports bar is a longtime local favorite for its weekend brunch and excellent burgers, not to mention the free-flowing beer. Grab a seat in the patio garden when the weather is fine.

Jáma
V jámě 7, New Town. Metro A, B: Můstek. 224 222 383. www.jamapub.cz.
An institution among the expat community, "The Hollow" has been serving burgers and beers in an American-style bar since 1994. Food here is hit or miss, but the music is always good. There's a good selection of brews on tap, and a garden out back.

Jo's Bar & Garage
Malostranské náměstí 7, Lesser Town. Trams 12 or 20: Malostranské náměstí. 257 531 422. www.josbar.cz.
Off the main square in the Lesser Town, Jo's Bar & Garage serves up pints and plates to an eclectic crowd of locals, expats and tourists. The friendly pub feel is enhanced by the long wooden bar and murals painted on the walls.

🚶 Letná Beer Garden
In Letná Park, Letná. Trams 1, 8, 15, 25 or 28: Letenské náměstí.
Prague has a plethora of beer gardens, but none can quite compare with the one in hilltop Letná Park *(see Parks and Gardens)*, the fairest of them all. Expect cheap beer in plastic cups, sausages hot off the grill, picnic tables and dogs running amok, and sweeping views over the city.

©Max Munson/Jáma

It's Always Time for Beer

While Pilsner Urquell may be the Czech Republic's best-known export, there's much more to Czech beer than the famous lager. More and more, beer drinkers are expanding their palates, and pubs are expanding their tap range to cater to the newfound interest in regional and craft brews. Many pubs will offer two or three types of beer, and the **Prague Beer Museum Pub** *(Dlouhá 46, Old Town; Metro B: Náměstí Republiky; 732 330 912; www.praguebeermuseum.com)* has 30 types on tap from across the country.

🍺 Pivovarský dům
Ječná/Lípová 15, New Town. Metro B: Karlovo náměstí. 296 216 666.

This microbrewery pours eight types of beer, ranging from its hopsy house pilsner to more daring concoctions such as chili beer and cherry beer. Copper tanks dominate the non-smoking room and decent snack food is on hand to sponge up the suds.

Tretter's
V kolkovně 7, Old Town. Metro A: Staroměstská. 224 819 089.

Having been rated on several world's-best lists in the past, Tretter's really knows its way around a cocktail – or around 200 of them, to be precise. Between the 150 classic mixed drinks and 50 house specialty cocktails, coupled with a hip vibe and a veritable Who's-Who clientele, you might not want to leave.

🍺 U Černého vola
Loretánské nám. 1, Hradčany. Trams 22 or 25: Pohořelec. 220 513 481.

Make a beeline for "The Black Ox," and do it early, as the intimate smoky space, long a Prague institution, fills up quickly with diehard fans. Don't look for great service; in fact, anticipate the opposite, which is part of the old-school charm here. And the excellent Kozel beer on tap is inexpensive to boot.

U Fleků
Křemencova 11, New Town. Metro B: Národní třída. 224 934 019. www.ufleku.cz.

Yes, U Fleků is usually packed with tourists, but it's still worth a stop. This microbrewery has been crafting beers for more than 500 years, and its rich and malty special dark lager goes down with a silky smoothness. Seating is at long, communal tables with wooden benches. Note the unique clock outside the door.

U Medvídků
Na Perštýně 7, Old Town. Metro B: Národní třída. 224 211 916. www.umedvidku.cz.

Another of the city's micro-breweries, "At the Bears" has several of its own varieties on tap. The brewery also holds Budvar, a convivial, warmly lit beer hall with a medieval feel and huge plates of Czech food. Choose a seat in the labyrinthine beer hall rooms, the sheltered garden, or the brewery.

🍴 Vinice Gazebo (Viniční altán)

Havlíčkovy sady 1369, Vinohrady. Trams 4 or 22: Krymská. 222 516 887. www.vinicni-altan.cz. For a romantic spot in which to sample regional wines and indulge in plates of cheese and sausage, settle in for an afternoon at this outdoor trellised wood pavilion. It overlooks hills of grapevines in its namesake vineyard in Vinohrady.

🍴 U Sudu

Vodičkova 10, New Town.
Tram 3, 9, 14 or 24: Vodičkova.
222 232 207. www.usudu.cz.
If your wine tastes stray toward more quantity, U Sudu is the place for you. Get lost in the web of subterranean stone-lined rooms, which house many a raucous special occasion. Lots of cheap wine, straight from the barrel to your carafe, fuels those late-night conversations.

U Veverky

Eliášova 14, Bubeneč. Metro A: Hradčanská. 223 000 223.
www.uveverky.com.
Consistently awarded the distinction of pouring the best Pilsner Urquell in Prague and ranking among the country's best pubs – a noteworthy feat – wood-lined U Veverky is worth a detour to the residential neighborhood of Bubeneč for a fresh pint and a friendly natter.

U Zlatého tygra

Husova 17, Old Town.
Metro A: Staroměstská.
www.uzlatehotygra.cz.
A tiger is the symbol of this authentic pub, where you can drink a pint to the memory of the late-20C Czech writer Bohumil Hrabal, who was a regular here. Come early, though; the popular place fills up quickly. Waiters pour an excellent Pilsner Urquell in a room decorated with stained-glass windows and Hrabal memorabilia.

Nightclubs

Cross Club

Plynární 26, Holešovice.
Metro C: Nádraží Holešovice.
736 535 053.
Whether you're into steam punk or just looking for a totally unique place, Cross Club has it all. Several levels of quirky mechanical decorations that transform scrap into art, cheap beer, late hours and a mix of ska, punk and reggae music brings 'em back for more.

🍴 Karlovy lázně

Smetanovo nábřeží, Old Town.
Metro A: Staroměstská. 222 220 502. www.karlovylazne.cz.
If one music club just isn't enough, Karlovy lázně, right next to the Charles Bridge, boasts five clubs spread out over five thumping floors, including a VIP all-inclusive area. The sound and light systems here, including the only three-color laser in the country, rank among the best in Europe.

MUST DO

That's the Spirit

In addition to beer, the Czechs have several favorite spirits. One of these is **slivovice**, plum brandy imbibed as a shot in bars and after a restaurant meal as a digestif. Many people distill their own at home for gifts and special occasions. **Becherovka**, which hails from the spa town of Karlovy Vary, is flavored with anise seed, cinnamon and a host of other herbs. Now used as bitters, Becherovka was originally marketed to relieve stomach pain.

Radost FX
Bělehradská 120, Vinohrady. Metro B: I.P. Pavlova. 603 193 711. www.radostfx.cz.
Arguably as popular for its weekend brunches in the colorful restaurant upstairs as for the lineup of DJs and bands that keep folks dancing downstairs, Radost FX lies just a few blocks' walk from Wenceslas Square. A rowdy crowd of regulars parties here to the sound of international bands.

Reduta Jazz Club
Národní třída 20, New Town. Metro B: Národní třída. 224 933 487. www.redutajazzclub.cz.
A local jazz legend, Reduta Jazz Club has been setting the city groove since it opened in 1957.

Reduta Jazz Club

© Lucas Vallecillos/age fotostock

Former President Bill Clinton even took to the stage on a saxophone here in 1994, treating audiences to an impromptu performance. In addition to jazz (of which there are live shows nightly starting at 9:30pm), Reduta also hosts theater productions, pantomime shows and black-light theater.

Roxy
Dlouhá 33, Old Town. Metro B: Náměstí Republiky. 602 691 015. www.roxy.cz.
The place to see or be seen at the latest indie concert or DJ set is Roxy, a local institution. There's something on every night of the week, and on Mondays there's no cover charge. Check out the modern gallery space, NoD, upstairs, often host to interactive exhibits or art performances.

Ungelt Jazz & Blues Club
Týnská ulička 2, Old Town. Metro A: Staroměstská. 224 895 787. www.jazzungelt.cz.
This tiny cellar space, just off Old Town Square, crams in as much atmosphere and good vibes as it does people on a regular night. Prop up at a table and order some dinner (it's a restaurant, too), and listen to the likes of the Luboš Andrst Blues Band, among others.

NIGHTLIFE

SPAS

Pounding the pavement can take its toll on you while on holiday, so why not treat yourself to a trip to one of Prague's renowned spas? Spas have a long tradition here, and their influence has affected the perception of spas as being not only relaxing, but vital to one's health. In fact, many Czech companies even subsidize their employees' visits to local spas, and owing to the fact that these facilities are so popular in Prague, many spas offer very affordable rates.

The Augustine Spa

*Augustine Hotel, Letenská 33/12/33, **Lesser Town**. Metro A: Malostranská. 266 112 272. www.theaugustine.com/spa-and-fitness.*

At this luxury hotel, an equally luxurious spa offers treatments and day packages to weary travelers, with a focus on a nature-inspired experience. Using secret recipes passed down by the Augustinian order of monks, the spa takes a holistic approach. Anika Organic Luxury products made from plant-based ingredients will revitalize your skin,

while the 90-minute signature Body Nourishing and Relaxing treatment starts with a soak in a Turkish bath and ends with a full-body massage.

Cybex Spa

*Hotel Hilton Prague, Pobřežní 1, **Karlin**. Trams 8 or 24: Karlínské náměstí. 224 842 375. www.cybex-fitness.cz.*

Whether you want to work out or chill out, you can do it at the Hilton's spa and fitness center. Boasting 2,000m²/21,527sq ft of space, the spa's facilities are complimentary to guests at the hotel, and day packages are available to non-guests. Before you relax with a Dead Sea salt peel or an Oriental mud wrap, try out some of the sports equipment. The extensive fitness center includes squash courts, an outdoor climbing wall, a swimming pool, Jacuzzi, Finnish sauna, and aerobics and yoga classes.

Health Club & Spa, InterContinental

*In the Hotel InterContinental, Pařížská 30, **Josefov**. Tram 17 Právnická fakulta. 296 631 525. www.icfitness.cz.*

Indulge in one of the fifteen types of massages offered here, ranging from traditional Swedish to chiropractic massage. Afterwards,

The Spa at Mandarin Oriental
©Mandarin Oriental Hotel Group

MUST DO

Spa Country

For a true local spa experience, visit the West Bohemian spa towns of **Karlovy Vary** or **Mariánské Lázně** *(see Excursions for both)*, where you can indulge in truly relaxing and medicinal treatments prescribed by onsite medical staff, or just lounge in the pools and partake of the healing thermal spring waters. Both towns have a variety of spa-package options that can be tailored to your desires.

keep those muscles limber in the dry Finnish sauna, then relax on deck chairs in the hotel's garden, where you can soak up some sun therapy. If you simply must have a workout, the adjoining fitness center has all the requisite weight and cardio equipment, in addition to a pool and Jacuzzi.

The Spa at Mandarin Oriental
In the Mandarin Oriental Hotel, Nebovidská 1, Lesser Town. Metro A Malostranská. 233 088 655. www.mandarinoriental.com/ prague/spa.
There's a reason this spa was voted Best Spa by readers of *Luxury Spa Finder* magazine. Schedule a half-day Bohemian Ritual here and you'll understand why. Incorporating reflexology principals, this treatment begins by resting your feet on warm pebbles and bathing them in water infused with fragrant oils. Clear out any stress with a stream shower and an aromatherapy massage; then enjoy spa cuisine for lunch. You'll leave glowing after the aromatherapy facial.

Thai World CZ
Na Můstku 1, Old Town. Metro A or B: Můstek. 224 225 710. www.thai-world.cz.
From one spa-rich culture to another, Thai massage parlors

have cropped up around Prague with much success. One of the largest is Thai World CZ, centrally located just off Wenceslas Square *(there's a second location at Karlova 22; metro A: Staromestska; 222 222 082).* Some of the practitioners here trained at the Thai Traditional Medicinal School, Wat Po, in Bangkok, and are skilled in traditional Thai techniques of body and foot massage. All this and reasonable prices: the Thai massage, for example, will run you a refreshing 420 Kč for 30 minutes.

Zoto Beer Spa
Masná 5, Old Town. Metro A: Staroměstská. 606 697 736. www.pivnilaznezoto.cz.
Beer has long been a popular tool in relaxation around these parts, so it's not surprising it has found its way into the bathtub – on purpose. More and more spas around the country are starting to offer beer-spa treatments, where you relax in Prague's liquid gold – in this case, water enriched with yeast, hops and other ingredients that go into beer. Poured into bathtubs that resemble wooden barrels, the bubbling beer bath is heated to temperatures above 35°C/89°F. You then soak in this mixture for 20 minutes. Think of it as a beer Jacuzzi.

RESTAURANTS

Long gone are the days when little else was to be found at Prague restaurants than pork and dumplings and surly service. The gastronomical scene has taken off in recent years, and the city boasts an array of cuisines in price ranges to suit any budget. Old Town and Lesser Town in particular are jam-packed with great restaurant options. While waiters may not be as chatty as their Western counterparts, and asking for substitutions in a dish is generally frowned upon, you can expect servers to speak multiple foreign languages and to be helpful and considerate.

Price and Amenities

The restaurants below were selected for their ambience, location, variety of regional dishes and/or value for money. Prices indicate the average cost of an appetizer, main course and dessert for one person, not including beverages, taxes or surcharges. Most restaurants are open daily (except where noted). Most, but not all, restaurants accept major credit cards.

When possible, reservations are a good idea; if a restaurant is full, most places don't encourage people to wait for a table. There are lingering instances of hidden charges being added to bills, so make sure to check the bill for anything that looks amiss. At some restaurants, particularly if you are dining in a group of six or more, a minimum service charge may be included; otherwise, leaving a tip of 10–15% is standard. When tipping, however, note it is customary to include the tip when paying, telling your waiter the total amount including the tip, as opposed to leaving cash on the table.

$ under 250 Kč
$$ 250–750 Kč
$$$ over 750 Kč

The Cuisine

Czech cuisine has seen a revival recently, putting aside its gloomy past and instead harking back to

Mistral Café

©Predrag Dukić/Mistral Café

its early 20C heyday. Czech fare borrows from other neighboring regional cuisines, with its own traditional versions of Hungarian and Austrian specialties. The most common dishes are beef goulash (*guláš*); beef tenderloin in cream sauce; pork schnitzel; and roast duck or goose (served quartered, halved or whole) with sauerkraut and bread dumplings. Other traditional dishes include *knedlo-vepřo-zelo*, made with pork and cabbage; and *svíčková nasmetaňe*, beef with cream and vegetables. *Knedlíky* is another must-taste when in Prague. These flour-and-egg or potato dumplings are leavened and steamed; the resulting bread-like dough is then cut into slices for serving. Though dessert is not customary after a meal in Prague (the Czechs prefer to have a slice of cake in the late afternoon at a café or tearoom), be sure to try the *palačinky*, thick pancakes stuffed with fruit (usually apples) and napped with rich chocolate sauce. If you just want a snack, pop into a pub for a beer and nibbles such as pickled Hermelin cheese, sausages and mustard, or pork lard cracklings that you can spread onto dense wheat bread.
Dobrou chuť!

Old Town

Bohemia Bagel
$ American
Masná 2. Metro A: Staroměstská. 224 812 560. www.bohemiabagel.cz.
With several locations around the city, Bohemia Bagel is a local institution appreciated for its freshly baked bagels, sandwiches, soups and burgers. With great

©Bohemia Bagel

breakfasts and weekend brunch specials, plus a special menu and a play area for kids, this chain is an ideal place to bring the whole family.

Kabul
$ Afghan
Karolíny Světlé 14. Metro B: Národní třída. 224 235 452.
www.kabulrestaurant.cz.
This quirky eatery is successful in both of its culinary endeavors: Afghan cuisine and pizza. Reasonable prices and large portions of kofta, kebabs, korma and the like satisfy diners, while the cramped interior opens out to a cozy courtyard garden out back.

Lokál
$ Czech
Dlouhá 33. Metro B: Náměstí Republiky. 222 316 265.
www.ambi.cz.
On the back of the Slow Food movement, this modern take on a traditional Czech pub transports local cuisine back to its roots and elevates the standards to exceptional heights. Classics like roast port, goulash, duck and fried cheese help soak up the freshly tapped Pilsner Urquell.

Mistral Café

$ Czech
Valentinská 11/56. Metro A: Staroměstská. 222 317 737. www.mistralcafe.cz.
Cheap and cheerful, Mistral Café goes to show that you don't have to sit in a dark, smoky pub to enjoy good Czech cuisine. This bright, modern, non-smoking space is a haven for everything from Czech classics to fish and chips. It's also an excellent spot to enjoy coffee and cake in the heart of Old Town.

Grosseto Marina

$$ Italian
Alšovo nábřeží. Metro A: Staroměstská. 605 454 020. www.grosseto.cz/marina.
For affordable and consistent pizza and Italian fare – not to mention the city's best view of Prague Castle – it doesn't get much better than this. The Grosseto chain has surpassed itself with this converted barge, providing ample indoor and covered outdoor seating.

Lehká hlava

$$ Vegetarian
Boršov 2. Metro A: Staroměstská. 222 220 665. www.lehkahlava.cz.
The whimsically designed restaurant, whose name translates to "Clear Head" in English, is proof that vegetarian food can be exciting. Expect eggplant quesadillas, Thai curry, burritos, salads, and mixed appetizer plates of tabouleh and hummus, among the inventive dishes that show off vegetables and legumes.

Lehká hlava

©René Jakl

Století

$$ International
Karolíny Světlé 21. Metro A: Staroměstská. 222 220 008. www.stoleti.cz.
Spiced-up beef and poultry dishes here take their names from famous personages, such as the William Somerset Maugham (rumpsteak with pepper sauce and banana slices) and the Al Capone (chicken leg with hot papaya salsa). Best of all, Století offers fine dining without breaking the bank.

U Závoje

$$ Mediterranean
Havelská 25. Metro A or B: Můstek. 226 006 109. www.uzavoje.cz.
Housed in the appropriately named House of Wines, U Závoje hosts regular wine-pairing events as well as a daily offering of wine-friendly snack plates and entrées (creamy truffle risotto; grilled sea bass with fennel and asparagus) influenced by French and Italian cuisines.

Bellevue

$$$ Continental
Smetanovo nábř. 18. Metro A: Staroměstská. 222 221 443. www.bellevuerestaurant.cz.
An upscale member of the esteemed V Zatisi group, Bellevue boasts rotating multicourse seasonal menus available either à la carte or in a prix-fixe chef's tasting. The restaurant's expert Wine Club

pairs wines with each dish, and the location, near Charles Bridge, is hard to beat.

Divinis

$$$ **Italian**

Týnská 21. Metro A: Staroměstská. 222 325 440. www.divinis.cz. Dinner only. Closed Sun.

A concise menu of Italian cheese and prosciutto plates, as well as multicourse offerings of inspired Mediterranean meats and pasta creations, makes Divinis a hit. An extensive wine list makes for long, happy evenings.

La Dégustation Bohême Bourgeoise

©La Degustation Bohême Bourgeoise

La Dégustation Bohême Bourgeoise

$$$ **Czech**

Haštalská 18. Metro B: Náměstí Republiky. 222 311 234. www.ladegustation.cz. No lunch Fri–Sat. Closed Sun and in July.

The Ambiente group's renowned La Dégustation is worth the hype – and the high prices. Settle in for several hours of course after course (seven in total) conceived by Executive Chef Oldřich Sahajdák, as he deconstructs and reconstitutes Czech cuisine into a world-class dining adventure.

La Finestra

$$$ **Italian**

Platněřská 90/13. Metro A: Staroměstská. 222 325 325. www.lafinestra.cz.

Fresh Italian dishes make for a luxurious experience at La Finestra, run by the same people as Aromi in Vinohrady. Meat gets priority on the menu here, with lusty veal, juicy steaks and truffles aplenty. The brick-lined interior creates a perfect backdrop for these and other seasonal plates.

Le Terroir

$$$ **Contemporary**

Jilská 6. Metro B: Národní třída. 222 220 260. Leterroir.cz. Closed Sun & Mon.

With a menu that changes every four weeks based on the freshest seasonal ingredients, this restaurant "of the land" is also of the times. Housed in a Romanesque brick cellar in the heart of the Old Town, Le Terroir offers the best of contemporary cuisine in an Old World atmosphere.

Mlýnec

$$$ **Czech**

Novotného lávka 9. Metro A: Staroměstská. 277 000 777. www.mlynec.cz.

Continental-inspired Czech dishes, such as beef tartare, crispy roast duck, and venison, take the classics to a new level here. The confident kitchen caters to one of the loveliest terraces in Prague, a stone's throw from the bustle and beauty of Charles Bridge.

RESTAURANTS

Sansho
$$$ **Asian Fusion**
Petrská 25. Metro A: Staroměstská.
222 317 425. www.sansho.cz.
No lunch Sat. Closed Mon.

Chef Paul Day created a new
sensation on the Prague dining
scene with the opening of
Sansho, with set menus of Asian
fusion delights served in a hip,
communal dining space in Old
Town. Reservations are a must for
the unforgettable beef redang
(cooked for 12 hours), among
other noteworthy dishes.

V Zátiší
$$$ **Continental**
Liliová 1. Metro B: Národní třída.
222 221 155. www.vzatisigroup.cz.

With both à la carte options and
a set tasting menu, the flagship
location of this restaurant and
catering group presents upscale
takes on Czech classics like *svíčková
na smetaně* (beef sirloin in cream
sauce) as well as pan-European
dishes. For dessert, why narrow your
choices? Go for the sampler plate.

Zinc
$$$ **Asian Fusion**
Hilton Prague Old Town, V Celnici 7.
Metro B: Náměstí Republiky. 221
822 300. www.hiltonprague
oldtown.com.

This sleek restaurant in the Hilton
(*see Must Stay*) consistently shows
innovation in the kitchen, with
Chef Ari Munander at the helm.
A native of Indonesia, Munander
whips up tasty signature dishes
such as roast duck in red curry
and spicy crispy prawns.

Castle Quarter

Lví dvůr
$$ **Czech**
U Prašného mostu 6. Tram 22:
Pražský hrad. 224 372 361.
www.lvidvur.cz.

Close to Prague Castle, Lví dvůr
claims some of the city's best-
quality Czech food, served in a
farmhouse-chic atmosphere in a
restored Renaissance-era house.
Try one of the restaurant's
specialties, like the roast suckling
pig or the veal Wiener Schnitzel
served with potato salad.

Bella Vista
$$$ **Continental**
Strahovské nádvoří 1. Tram 22:
Pohořelec. 220 517 274.
www.kolkovna.cz.

True to its name, Bella Vista boasts
magnificent views over the city,
from its idyllic location in the
Strahov Monastery, between
Prague Castle and Petřín Hill. Prices
are accordingly high for the likes of
Czech kettle goulash and roasted
lamb with onion-mustard sauce,
but the experience is well worth
the splurge.

U Zlaté hrušky
$$$ **Continental**
Nový svět 3. Tram 22: Pražský hrad.
220 941 244. www.restaurant
uzlatehrusky.cz.

One of Prague's most beautiful
restaurants, U Zlaté hrušky boasts
an elegant dining room with a
beamed barrel-vaulted ceiling.
Located on the magical New World
(Nový svět) cobbled street just off
Castle Square, The Golden Pear's
talented kitchen has long upheld
its reputation for excellence.

MUST EAT

Jewish Town

Les Moules
$$ **Belgian**
Pařížská 19. Tram 17: Pravnická fakulta. 222 315 022.
www.lesmoules.cz.
The famed mussels of Brussels have found a happy home in Prague's Jewish Town. Large pots of the crustaceans come in a variety of tempting preparations, with a solid selection of additional seafood dishes and Belgian specialties rounding out the mix. Of course, there are plenty of Belgian beers on tap to pair with your meal.

Pepe Nero
$$ **Italian**
Bílkova 6. Tram 17: Pravnická fakulta. 222 315 543. Pepenero.cz.
Pepe Nero serves some of the best pizza in Prague, made with imported fresh Bufala mozzarella and expertly crafted *sugo* (sauce). Cracker-thin crusts and reasonable prices make this a popular standby for locals and visitors alike.

Lesser Town

Café Lounge
$ **International**
Plaská 8. Trams 6, 9, 12, 20 or 22: Újezd. 257 404 020. www.cafe-lounge.cz. Closes at 5pm Sun.
Despite securing the title of "Best Café 2010" in the Czech Bar Awards, this cozy café still feels like a secret. Tucked into a side street near the bottom of Petřín Hill, it serves up excellent breakfast and brunch options daily, as well as a modest but winning menu of daily specials.

Artisan
$$ **International**
Rošických 4. Trams 6, 9, 12 or 20: Újezd. 257 218 277.
www.artisanrestaurant.cz.
The American chef at Artisan, just off the tourist trails at the bottom of Petřín Hill, prepares a confident mix of classics, like the hickory-smoked burger, as well as dishing up house-baked bread and freshly made pastas in an intimate space.

Cowboys
$$ **Steakhouse**
Nerudova 40. Metro A: Malostranská. 296 826 107.
www.kampagroup.com.
Steaks – in every size and form – are the name of the game here, served up with your choice of sauces and sides (like homemade fries and grilled tomatoes). The sprawling patio terrace has some of the district's best views over the red-slate rooftops and church spires of the Lesser Town.

Luka Lu
$$ **Balkan**
Újezd 33. Trams 12, 20 or 22: Hellichova. 257 212 388.
www.lukalu.cz.
It's worth visiting Luka Lu for the décor alone: colorful, dream-inspired art crosses from paintings to birdcages to fanciful furniture, spilling out into a magical garden out back – complete with a treehouse table for diners lucky enough to score it. Of course, the inspired Balkan cooking wins its share of raves too.

RESTAURANTS

Nebozízek
$$ Continental
*Petřínské sady 411. Funicular
from Újezd. 257 315 329.
www.nebozizek.cz.*
Up in the well-kept wilds of
Petřín Hill, Nebozízek is an oasis
of grandeur overlooking the city.
Accessible either by the funicular
or the paths that wind through
the park, this chateau/restaurant is
about as romantic as it gets.

Nebozízek
©Nebozízek

Olympia
$$ Czech
*Vítězná 7. Trams 6, 9, 12 or 20:
Újezd. 251 511 080.
www.kolkovna.cz.*
Olympia revels in well-crafted
Czech pub food, serving up beer
snacks, pickled sausages, pork,
goose, and the mighty Bohemian
platter: a bit of everything, served
with sauerkraut and dumplings.
And of course, there's plenty of
Pilsner Urquell on tap to wash it
all down.

Villa Richter
$$-$$$ Continental
*Staré zámecké schody 6. Metro A:
Malostranská. 257 219 079.
www.villarichter.cz.*
Right off the Castle Steps, this
complex inside a converted
villa contains three restaurants

catering to different budgets.
This way, there's something for
everyone to enjoy, along with
the views over the castle gardens
and beyond.

Ada
$$$ Continental
*Hotel Hoffmeister, Pod Bruskou 7.
Metro A: Malostranská. 251 017
111. www.hoffmeister.cz.*
In the Hotel Hoffmeister, delicacies
such as veal sweetbreads and foie
gras compete for your attention
with the local art exhibited on
the walls. With a secluded garden
perfect for the summer months,
Ada also boasts a good location
close to the Castle Steps.

Alchymist Garden
$$$ Continental
*Nosticova 1. Metro A:
Malostranská. 257 312 518.
www.alchymist.cz.*
Gilded and grand from plate
to ceiling, Alchymist Garden
truly understands the value of
gold. Zebra-print chairs, ornate
chandeliers and a lavish namesake
garden complement the seafood
dishes and meats on the carefully
conceived menu.

Coda
$$$ Continental
*Aria Hotel, Tržiště 9. Trams 12, 20
or 22: Malostranské náměstí. 225
334 761. www.codarestaurant.cz.*
In the aptly named Aria Hotel,
Coda hits the high notes (and the
high prices) with its à la carte and
chef's tasting menus. Luxury and
comfort food mingle here, along
the lines of filet mignon, duck
confit and fois gras, as well as
upscale Czech favorites.

MUST EAT

Essensia

$$$ Asian

*Mandarin Oriental Prague,
Nebovidská 1. Metro A:
Malostranská. 233 088 888.
www.mandarinoriental.cz.*

Asian fare meets a loving
reinvention of Czech cuisine
in these minimalist, vaulted-
ceilinged rooms, with an ample
wine selection and focus on both
precision and luxury. Pineapple
curry with coconut salad and
yakisoba noodles with sautéed
beef share the menu with local pike
perch and roasted suckling pig.

Hergetova Cihelna

$$$ International

*Cihelná 2b. Metro A: Malostranská.
296 826 103. www.kampagroup.com.*

You'd be hard-pressed to find a
nicer place from which to admire
Charles Bridge and the spires
of Old Town than the terrace of
this riverside restaurant. One of
the city's most beautiful interiors
matches the skillful version of
Caesar salad, chicken tikka masala
and tempura fried tuna, among
other tempting dishes.

Kampa Park

$$$ International

*Na Kampě 8b. Trams 12, 20 or
22: Hellichova. 296 826 112.
www.kampagroup.com.*

The flagship restaurant of the
renowned Kampa Group is located
on lush Kampa Island, close to the
Charles Bridge and within easy
reach of the Lesser Town sights.
One of the city's first real
destination restaurants, Kampa
Park pairs the likes of steamed
salmon roll and stuffed chicken
breast with 150 different labels
of wine.

Palffý Palác

©Palffý Palác

Palffý Palác

$$$ Continental

*Valdštejnská 14. Metro A:
Malostranská. 257 530 522.
www.palffy.cz.*

For great views and a baroque
atmosphere befitting the history of
the Lesser Town, Palffý is the place.
The converted palace, located
within easy distance of Prague
Castle, combines timeless elegance
with a modern palate, serving
items such as seared yellowfin
tuna and "Bavette" beef flank.

U Modré kachničky

$$$ Czech

*Nebovidská 6. Trams 12, 20,
22 Hellichova. 257 320 308.
www.umodrekachnicky.cz.*

Game snares all the attention here.
Start with a rich paté and work your
way through any number of duck
dishes, or sample the roast wild
boar, saddle of fallow deer, and
roast pheasant or hare. As you'd
expect, the décor is fittingly rustic.

U Zlaté studně

$$$ Continental

*U Zlaté studně 4. Metro A:
Malostranská. 257 533 322.
www.terasauzlatestudne.cz.*

A high standard of luxury meets
unrivaled views over the Lesser
Town here. Delectable seasonal

menus, both à la carte and dégustation, list dishes that venture slightly into fusion fare while remaining grounded in fine continental ingredients.

New Town

V Cípu

$ **Czech**

V cípu 1. Metro A or B: Můstek. 607 177 107. www.restauracevcipu.cz.
Large portions and low prices – not to mention the convivial Czech pub atmosphere and the restaurant's location just off Wenceslas Square – make V Cípu an open secret. For a real treat, tackle the quarter roast duck, which comes with sauerkraut and two types of dumplings for under 100 Kc. To wash it down, go for the excellent Breznak beer, among the other local quaffs on tap here.

Botel Matylda

$$ **Italian**

Boathotel Matylda, Masarykovo nabrezi. Trams 14 or 17: Jiraskovo náměstí. 222 511 826. www.botelmatylda.cz.
Enjoy Prague's charming views with a touch of Mediterranean elegance at this boat hotel's restaurant, where you can bask on deck or in the classy ship-shape port room and take in the panorama while sipping Prosecco and tucking into fresh pasta and regional specialties.

Café Louvre

$$ **International**

Národní 22. Metro B: Národní třída. 224 930 949. cafelouvre.cz.
A Prague institution, Café Louvre deserves as much attention for the quality of its food as for its Art Nouveau interior and celebrated past patrons (Franz Kafka and Albert Einstein, for example). Burgers, omelets, salads and sandwiches hold sway here – not to mention cake and coffee plus a good weekend brunch.

Červená tabulka

$$ **Continental**

Lodecká 4. Metro B: Náměstí Republiky. 224 810 401. www.cervenatabulka.cz.
Adorable, whimsically inspired farmhouse-style rooms make for a romantic, intimate visit to "The Red Tablet," where small touches elevate simple dishes to excellence. The idyllic courtyard entrance turns into an ideal haven in warmer months.

Čestr

$$ **Steakhouse**

Legerova 75/57. Metro A or C: Muzeum. 222 727 851. www.ambi.cz.
Here's a novel idea: a restaurant dedicated to different cuts of aged Czech beef. With an airy, stylish dining hall close to the National Museum, and hearty steaks served on wooden chopping boards, Čestr has a good thing going.

Cicala

$$ **Italian**

Žitná 43. Metro B: Karlovo náměstí. 222 210 375. www.trattoria.cicala.cz.
Authentic homestyle Italian cooking comes courtesy of the Cicala family at this cozy trattoria. Tucked away on a busy street, Cicala is memorable both for its ambience and buffet. Pictures of celebrity patrons line the walls, and wine and good cheer abound.

Como

$$ Mediterranean

*Václavské náměstí 45. Metro A
or C: Muzeum. 222 247 240.
www.comorestaurant.cz.*

Amid the hawkers and camera-
slung throngs of Wenceslas Square,
Como is a classy place with prices
surprisingly low for such an
enviable address. Feast on the likes
of sea bream with roast vegetables,
and duck confit with red cabbage
and potato dumplings while
watching people pass through the
square. Tune in for jazzy live music
inside come evening.

Como

©COMO Restaurant & Café

La Rotonde

$$ Continental

*Stepanska 40. Metro A or B: Můstek.
222 820 410. www.alcron.cz/html/
la_rotonde.html.*

Like its neighboring restaurant
Alcron, La Rotonde is under the
auspices of Chef Roman Paulus.
The restaurant offers a skilled and
affordable menu of the chef's
interpretation of local favorites,
such as *svickova* and Schnitzel, as
well as pan-European specialties
with unique twists.

Oliva

$$ Mediterrranean

*Plavecká 4. Metro B: Karlovo
náměstí. 222 520 288. www.oliva
restaurant.cz. Sat dinner only.
Closed Sun.*

A block up from the Vltava River
and on the way to Vyšehrad
Cathedral, Oliva specializes in a
mélange of Mediterranean cuisine
– from eggplant parmigiana to
mussels marinière – with a focus
on freshness. For the budget-
conscious, prices are a fraction of
those found at restaurants closer
to the city center.

Resto Café Patio

$$ International

*Národní 22. Metro B: Národní třída.
224 934 375. www.lepatio.cz.*

This restaurant cum interior-design
shop understands beauty, both on
the plate and on the walls. Lanterns
dangle over tables where diners
tuck into pasta, burgers, salads
and steaks, spiked by a hint of the
exotic throughout.

Ultramarin

$$ International

*Ostrovn í 32. Metro B: Národní
třída. 224 932 249.
www.ultramarin.cz.*

A stylish hangout renowned both
for its music club downstairs and
its eclectic high-quality food: baba
ganoush, Thai curries, steaks off
the lava grill, and the mighty
"Elvis King" burger.

Výtopna

$$ Czech

*Václavské nám. 56. Metro A or
C: Muzeum. 725 190 646. praha.
vytopna.cz.*

Výtopna is sure to please both
young and old, with a model train
system that runs throughout the
sprawling restaurant, delivering
drinks to the tables. Czech classics
are admirably handled here, and

the place has some of the cheapest beer to be found this side of the tracks on Wenceslas Square.

Žofín Garden
$$ International
Slovanský ostrov. Metro B: Národní třída. 774 774 774.
www.zofingarden.cz.
Attached to the beautiful Žofín Chateau on an island on the Vltava, Žofín Garden is sheltered in all seasons. Here you can enjoy views over the river, a beautiful dining gazebo, a great play area for kids and, best of all, reasonably priced international dishes from the well-regarded Žofín catering group.

Alcron
$$$ Seafood
Stepanska 40. Metro A or B: Můstek. 224 948 039. www.alcron.cz.
Dinner only (lunch available by request). Closed Sat & Sun.
Alcron has long been *the* destination in Prague for seafood, thanks to Chef Roman Paulus. The 24-seat dining room allows you to appreciate the feat of preparing delectable langoustines, halibut and more in a landlocked country.

Francouzská restaurace Obecní dům
$$$ French
Náměstí Republiky 5. Metro B: Náměstí Republiky. 222 002 770. francouzskarestaurace.cz.
Ornate Municipal House contains this equally grand French restaurant, complete with gilded walls and Art Nouveau accents. High culture meets well-prepared haute cuisine here, in halls frequented by international dignitaries and celebrities.

Le Grill
$$$ Continental
Hybernská 12. Metro B: Náměstí Republiky. 226 226 126.
www.kempinski.com.
A luxurious place to relax over lunch or dinner, at Le Grill you can dine on the likes of duck confit or braised leg of lamb in elegant surroundings, just steps from the Powder Tower and Náměstí Republiky.

Greater Prague

Las Adelitas
$ Mexican
Americká 8, Vinohrady. Metro A: Náměstí Míru. 222 542 031.
www.lasadelitas.cz.
The thought of authentic Mexican food in Prague seemed like a dream a few short years ago, but with Las Adelitas on the scene, it's now a happy reality. This tiny, Mexican-run place packs in the crowds for its pitchers of margaritas, extensive tequila list and tacos *al pastor*.

The Pind
$ Indian
Korunní 67, Vinohrady. Metro A: Jiriho z Podebrad. 222 516 085.
www.thepind.cz.
This place created quite a stir when it opened, exciting all curry lovers with its authentic Indian and Pakistani dishes and oh-so-reasonable prices. The lunch buffet (109 Kč) includes rice, a chicken dish, daal and all the trimmings: salad, raita, poppadams and naan.

Svijanský rytíř
$ Czech
Jirečkova 13, Holešovice. Trams 1, 8, 15, 25 or 26: Letenské náměstí. 233 378 342. restaurace-svijanskyrytir.wz.cz.

A classic Czech pub, Svijanský rytíř is dedicated to its crisp regional namesake lager, Svijany. With several different types on tap, it's tempting to try them all, but not before you fuel up on the well-executed pub food.

Aromi
$$ Italian
Mánesova 78, Vinohrady. Metro A: Jiřího z Poděbrad. 222 713 222. www.aromi.cz.
The über-trendy neighborhood of Vinohrady is home to cozy Aromi, a longtime Italian favorite. Here, house-made pastas vie with fresh fish, brought to the table pre-cooked for viewing.

Mozaika
$$ International
Nitranská 13, Vinohrady. Metro A: Jiřího z Poděbrad. 224 253 011. www.restaurantmozaika.cz.
For dining out near the border of hip Vinohrady and even hipper Žižkov, Mozaika is beloved for its burger, which comes on a house-made spinach bun, and always ranks among Prague's best.

Perpetuum
$$ Czech
Na Hutích 9, Bubeneč. Metro A: Dejvická. 233 323 429. www.restauraceperpetuum.cz.
Perpetuum is a love song to all things duck, from patés and seared livers to roasted and grilled meat with a variety of sauces. This place is a must for all lovers of Czech cuisine's favorite feathered friend.

SaSaZu
$$ Asian
Bubenské nábřeží 13, Holešovice. Trams 1, 3 or 5: Pražská tržnice. 284
097 455. www.prague.sasazu.com.
Super-hip SaSaZu, a glitzy restaurant/club, has Prague head over heels. A chic atmosphere complements tasty fusion fare like chicken dim sum and the addictive Hanoi shrimp.

Taverna Olympos
$$ Greek
Kubelíkova 9, Žižkov. Metro A: Jiriho z Podebrad. 222 722 239. www.taverna-olympos.eu.
Olympos manages to transport you to the Mediterranean from this hip residential neighborhood. Bountiful mezze platters brim with fresh grilled meats, seafood and Greek specialties, while the Retsina flows freely. Celebrate a summer night in the expansive back garden.

CzecHouse
$$$ Czech
Hilton Prague, Pobřežní 1, Karlín. Trams 8 or 24: Karlínské náměstí. 224 841 111. www.hiltonprague.com.
This grill and rotisserie adds contemporary flair to traditional regional cuisine, as well as serving quality steaks with continental accents. Located in the Hilton Prague, CzecHouse makes an upscale meal out of local classics.

Da Emanuel
$$$ Italian
Charlese de Gaulla 4, Bubeneč. Metro A: Hradčanská. 224 312 934. Daemanuel.cz.
One of the city's best Italian eateries, Da Emanuel boasts the unforgettable culinary whims of its owner, Italian-born celebrity chef Emanuele Ridi. The intimate room, with arched brick walls, encourages lingering over drinks long after the plates have been cleared.

RESTAURANTS

HOTELS

There's no shortage of options for accommodations in Prague, and every neighborhood is full of them. The city center – Old Town, New Town and Lesser Town – all boast luxurious hotels as well as more modest pensions, guesthouses and hostels. If you're in Prague only for a few days, the city center is a good place to stay, as you'll be within walking distance to the museums and historic sites you'll want to visit. If you plan to spend a longer stretch of time exploring the city, consider staying in the residential areas of Vinohrady or Žižkov, which are considerably less expensive and offer more opportunities to rent an apartment. *The peak tourist seasons are April–May and September–October. Hotel prices tend to be lower from June–August.*

Prices and Amenities

The hotels and guesthouses described here are classified according to the price for a **double room** in high season for one night, not including taxes or surcharges. Since these prices often vary considerably throughout the year, inquire beforehand and check the rates during the period chosen for your stay. Many of the hotels featured in this guide also have first-class spas and restaurants *(see Spas and Must Eat)*.

The hotels listed in this guide are open year-round, except when otherwise stated. Most hotels in Prague accept payment by credit card, with Visa and MasterCard being accepted in most places. Many hotels also take American Express and Diners cards, but these are less widely accepted, so be sure to check in advance. Depending on the time of year, hotels may offer special package rates; check the website before you go to see if they have any current deals.

$ under 1,500 Kč
$$ 1,500-2,500 Kč
$$$ 2,500-3,750 Kč
$$$$ 3,750-5,000Kč
$$$$$ over 5,000 Kč

Online Booking

The majority of the hotels listed in this guide allow for online booking through their websites.

Alchymist Residence Nosticova, p 148

©Alchymist Residence Nosticova

MUST STAY

Where this is not available, you can also try making reservations through websites such as **www.bookings.com** or the other sites listed below. The official Prague Tourism Board website – **www.praguewelcome. cz/en** – has a comprehensive hotel, hostel and pension directory with addresses and contact information.

Reservations Websites

Alternatively, you can book hotel rooms while checking out the reviews from other travelers on the following websites:

* www.wotif.com
* www.hotels.com
* www.expedia.com
* www.ebookers.com
* www.prague-hostels.cz

Old Town

Old Prague Hostel
$ 17 rooms
Benediktská 2. 224 829 058. www.oldpraguehostel.com.
Located in the historical center of Prague and highly rated by Hostels.com and other consumer-review-based websites, this affordable, tidy hostel offers rooms with two to eight beds; all have shared bathrooms. Breakfast is included in the price, as are Wi-Fi access, linens, towels, hairdryers and lockers in every dormitory, making this a perfect place to stay for anyone watching their budget.

Attractive Penzion
$$ 10 rooms
Smetanovo nábřeží 14. 222 220 495. www.attractivepenzion.cz.
Set right in the center of Old Town, this lovely, small historic hotel overlooks the Vltava River

©Rod Purcell/Apa Publications

Betlem Club

and boasts a great view of the towers of Prague Castle. Attractive Penzion also offers an apartment with a fully equipped kitchen and whirlpool tub as well as rooms with a private or shared bathroom. On the ground floor, the café/bar **Atmosphere ($)** proves a popular spot with students and tourists alike. A buffet breakfast is included in the rate.

Betlem Club Hotel
$$ 21 rooms
Betlémské náměstí 9. 222 221 574-5. www.betlemclub.cz.
The most important sights of Old Town – places such as Charles Bridge, the National Theater, Old Town Square, Wenceslas Square, the Royal Route and the Jewish Town – surround the Betlem Club Hotel. For the affordable price, you'll get a clean and tidy room, a buffet breakfast, and access to laundry and babysitting services. As an added bonus, the hotel offers its own car service with transport to and from the airport or the train station, though this is not included in the room rate. Pick-up from the airport costs 650 Kč for one car (one to four persons), and 960 Kč for two cars (five to eight persons).

HOTELS

Central Hotel
$$ 51 rooms
Rybná 8. 222 317 220.
www.central-prague.com.
Located on the quiet side street of Rybna in Old Town, Central Hotel is very close to many of Prague's most famous attractions. Built in 1931, the hotel is also within walking distance of some of the best shopping in Prague. Central offers free Internet access, smoking rooms upon request, room service, and a free hot and cold buffet breakfast to its guests.

Pension Corto
$$ 10 rooms
Havelská 15. 224 215 313.
www.corto.cz.
Although the market held every day in front of this beautiful Renaissance-style manor in the heart of the Old Town can be boisterous, you'll have fresh local produce, flowers and crafts right at your doorstep. If peace and quiet is a priority, request one of the newly renovated attic rooms on the fifth floor, which also offer the best views. All rooms have private baths and come equipped with free Wi-Fi and satellite TV. Downstairs, the **Corto Restaurant/Pizzeria ($$)** offers a 20-percent discount to guests of the hotel. Car service is available to and from the airport or train station (not included in the room rate; pick-up from the airport costs 550 Kč for one car and 700 Kč for two cars).

Grand Majestic Plaza Hotel
$$$ 196 rooms
Truhlářská 16. 211 159 100.
www.hotel-grandmajestic.cz.
A member of the WORLDHOTELS chain, the Grand Majestic Plaza is perfect for a quick getaway in Prague, as it offers luxurious rooms and a great location at reasonable prices. If you need to relax, check out the hotel's health suite, which includes a sauna and whirlpool, as well as a Thai massage center and a salon. Four conference rooms, all with excellent natural light, accommodate up to 260 people. Air-conditioned rooms offer extras like mini-bars, coffee-makers and safe deposit boxes, while each of the six suites has its own balcony. Wi-Fi connection and a buffet breakfast are included in the rates.

Old Town Square Hotel
$$$ 10 rooms
Staroměstské náměstí 20. 221 421 111. www.otsh.com.
As the name suggests, this hotel is situated right on Old Town Square. With views of the square and the surrounding landmarks from your room, hotels don't get much more central than this. Spacious, recently renovated guest quarters are done in clean, contemporary lines and colors (mostly black and white with red accents). There's even a guarded parking lot, and breakfast is included in the room rate. The hotel's Jazz and Blues Lounge Bílý Koníček features live music on a regular basis.

Grand Hotel Bohemia
$$$$ 78 rooms
Králodvorská 4. 234 608 111.
www.grandhotelbohemia.cz.
Located next to the Powder Tower at the beginning of the Royal Route, this boutique hotel boasts newly renovated and immaculately kept rooms done in dark woods and light colors. Bathrooms

have heated floors. And there's a splendid neo-Baroque ballroom for special events. The friendly, professional staff can help arrange tours, make dining reservations, and suggest fun things to do while you're in Prague. For lunch and dinner, the **Restaurant Franc Josef ($$$)** specializes in gourmet Bohemian fare.

Hilton Prague Old Town
$$$$ 303 rooms
V Celnici 7. 221 822 100.
www.hiltonpragueoldtown.com.
Blending Art Deco style with a modern look, the Hilton in Old Town (there is another Hilton in Karlín) offers all the amenities that you would expect from this world-wide chain. Rooms combine style and comfort with large windows that open, while the recently renovated fitness center includes a gym and an indoor swimming pool. Also situated in the hotel, **Zinc Restaurant** ($$$; *see Must Eat*) serves Asian-inspired cuisine.

Savic Hotel
$$$$ 27 rooms
Jilská 7. 224 248 555.
www.savichotelprague.com.
Hidden within the labyrinthine cobbled lanes that mark the Old Town, Savic Hotel occupies a Gothic-style building, some parts of which date back to the 12C. Despite its long history, the hotel claims all the major modern conveniences like air-conditioning and free Internet connection in the rooms (Wi-Fi is available in the public spaces). Mahogany furniture, parquet floors, and crystal chandeliers set a sumptuous scene in the guest rooms.

A complimentary buffet breakfast is served each morning in the hotel's restaurant, whose outdoor terrace makes a lovely place for an alfresco meal in summer.

Four Seasons Prague
$$$$$ 161 rooms
Veleslavínova 2a. 221 427 000.
www.fourseasons.com/prague.
Luxury is a matter of course at the Prague outpost of this renowned chain. With views over the Vltava to Charles Bridge and Prague Castle, the Four Seasons is ideally situated. Rooms and suites are spread over three historic buildings, which are joined by a new contemporary structure. Marble bathrooms come with a deep soaking tub and separate glass shower, while high-tech amenities include flat-screen TVs, iPod connections and Wi-Fi Internet access throughout. Room service is available, and a complimentary buffet breakfast is

Four Seasons Prague

© Peter Vitale/Four Seasons Hotels and Resorts

included. Two private treatment rooms in the on-site fitness center offer limited spa services.

Jewish Town

Pension Accord
$$ 11 rooms
Rybná 9. 222 328 816.
www.accordprague.com.
This hotel is a win-win, with low prices, cheery well-kept rooms that let in lots of natural light, and peace and quiet, all only a few steps from the central monuments of the city. Free Internet connection is included in the rates, as is a buffet breakfast served in Red Hot and Blues restaurant right across the street. Ask the helpful English-speaking staff at the reception desk to arrange tours, ticket reservations and rental cars.

President Hotel Prague
$$$ 130 rooms
Námesti Curieových 100. 234 614 111. www.hotelpresident.cz.
Sitting on the banks of the Vltava River within walking distance of the main sites of the Jewish Town, the President Hotel Prague offers both smoking and non-smoking rooms equipped with comforts like a hair dryer, safe, iron and

ironing board, and bathrobes and air-conditioning. Wi-Fi access is free throughout the property, and breakfast is included in the rates for select rooms. Also onsite is a spa with a sauna, Jacuzzi and a Thai massage center offering countless possibilities for relaxation. Golfers, take note: the staff here can make reservations for tee times at various golf courses throughout Prague and beyond.

InterContinental Prague
$$$$$ 372 rooms
Pařížská 30. 296 631 111.
www.icprague.com.
Part of a respected worldwide luxury chain, the InterContinental Prague is one of the most upscale hotels to be found in the city. There's an indoor saltwater pool and a luxurious spa if you want to unwind, and the on-site business center obliges if you must work. Rooms are contemporary and comfortable, outfitted with down comforters and work desks. On the rooftop, **Zlatá Praha ($$$)** restaurant dishes up seasonal cuisine along with spectacular views of the skyline. The hotel also offers conference rooms to accommodate those who are in town on business.

President Hotel Prague

©President Hotel Prague

InterContinental Prague

©Rod Purcell/Apa Publications

Lesser Town

Charles Hotel
$$ 31 rooms
Josefská 1. 774 644 466 or 211 151 300. www.hotel-charles.cz.
This luxury hotel is ideal for a romantic getaway in the Golden City. Rooms are tastefully done with dark woods and painted ceilings. You will find the small staff extremely attentive and accommodating; the hotel even accepts pets for an extra fee. Located just off Charles Bridge, the hotel is convenient to a plethora of bars, cafes and restaurants. Breakfast is included in the price of the room.

Hotel Neruda
$$ 42 rooms
Nerudova 44. 257 535 557 61. www.hotelneruda.cz.
Hotel Neruda is another one of Malá Strana's hotels that is perfect for those weekends away for two. Reasonably priced and located on the road leading directly to both the castle and Charles Bridge, the Neruda offers special weekend packages that include spa treatments and romantic meals for two on the hotel restaurant's terrace. Walls in the standard rooms

are decorated with excerpts of poems from Czech poet Jan Neruda.

Best Western Hotel Kampa
$$$ 84 rooms
Všehrdova 16. 257 404 444. www.hotel-kampa.info.
Just off Kampa Park , the hotel is situated on one of the more peaceful corners of the Lesser Town. Expect good service and clean, affordable rooms at this well-respected global hotel chain. The on-site restaurant, **The Knights Hall ($$$)**, located in a grand room beneath the hotel, is decked out in medieval décor. Breakfast is included in the price of the room, and room service is available from 7am until 10pm.

Hotel Red Lion
$$$ 9 rooms
Nerudova 41. 257 533 832. www.hotelredlion.cz.
This 15C building sits on the cobbled Royal Route in the heart of the Lesser Town. With its antique furniture and original, painted wooden ceilings dating to the 17C, the Red Lion perfectly complements the Renaissance architecture of Prague. All rooms have stunning views of Petřín Hill and the red rooftops of the Lesser Town. The hotel's historic pub, U Červeného Lva, located in a limestone cellar below the hotel, makes a cozy place for a beer.

Pension Dientzenhofer
$$$ 9 rooms
Nosticova 2. 257 311 319. www.dientzenhofer.cz.
Once the residence of Kilian Ignac Dientzenhofer, a noted Prague architect, this pension boasts a quiet location in the Lesser Town.

The rooms are simple, clean and bright, and amenities include laundry and dry-cleaning services, a complimentary buffet breakfast, and even car service to and from the airport. A friendly staff and a charming little courtyard are just two more reasons to stay here.

Hotel Čertovka
$$$$ 21 rooms
U lužického semináře 2/85. 257 011 500. www.certovka.cz.
This recently refurbished Baroque-style house is a stone's throw from Charles Bridge. With a multitude of bars, cafes and historic sites within walking distance of the hotel, the Čertovka is well-situated for both sightseeing and mingling with the locals. The hotel's rooms all feature air-conditioning, and a buffet breakfast is included in the rate.

Santini Residence
$$$$ 12 rooms
Nerudova 14/211. 257 195 111. www.santiniresidence.com.
Most of the guestrooms in this romantic 17C property boast lovely painted coffered ceilings, and all have wood parquet floors, Persian carpets and marble baths. LCD TV, CD and DVD player and a robe and slippers add to the creature comforts. For guests' convenience, the reception staff is available 24 hours a day. Breakfast, which can be served in your room or in the hotel breakfast area, is not included in the price of the room.

Alchymist Residence Nosticova
$$$$$ 16 rooms
Nosticova 1. 257 312 513. www.nosticova.com.
On a cobblestone side street near Kampa Park, this 17C residence names each of its 16 suites after a different figure from Czech history. You'll feel like royalty in rooms rich with gilded furniture, plush bedding and crystal chandeliers. If you need to relax, avail yourself of the spa at the hotel's sister property, a few doors down the street. The hotel's **restaurant ($$$)** occupies a secluded garden.

Aria Hotel
$$$$$ 52 rooms
Tržiště 9. 225 334 111. www.ariahotel.net.
This award-winning hotel is one of the most luxurious in Prague. True to its name, the hotel features rooms that are each dedicated to a specific style of music, with each floor being arranged around a different genre, from classical

Santini Residence

©Santini Residence

Aria Hotel

©Aria Hotel Prague

to contemporary. All the rooms include an iPod with more than 500 songs. There's also a screening room for movies, a fitness center and a beauty salon onsite. Plan a dinner at **Coda ($$$)** for a fine-dining experience in unique Art Deco surroundings.

New Town

Chili Hostel
$ 24 rooms
Pštrossova 205/7. 603 119 113.
www.chili.dj.
Perfect for backpackers and budget travelers, Chili Hostel is clean and centrally located. Here, you will be close to many of the city sights as well as great pubs and nightclubs in Prague. The hostel offers private and shared rooms, all with a shared bathroom. Breakfast is available in the morning for 73 Kč, and guests have access to a shared kitchen. Cash in Czech crowns is the only method of payment accepted here.

Pension Alabastr
$$ 21 rooms
Školská 20. 296 325 016 or 602 321 716. www.pensionalabastr.cz.
These spacious studios are a good value, especially since each comes with its own kitchen and Wi-Fi

access. The garden in the back is open to guests, and the staff will bring the continental breakfast to your room upon request. If you're looking for rest and relaxation, request a room on one of the upper floors (lower floors tend to be noisy).

Hotel City Bell
$$ 20 rooms
Belgická 10. 222 522 422.
www.hotelcitybell.cz.
Close to Náměstí Míru and near the border with Vinohrady, this hotel offers clean, inexpensive accommodations. In addition to single, double and triple rooms, the City Bell has apartments that can sleep up to five people. A buffet breakfast is included.

Hotel Christie
$$$ 135 rooms
Vladislavova 20. 246 091 700.
www.hotelchristie.cz.
Just a few blocks from Wenceslas Square, the Christie offers modern, comfortable and clean rooms as well as several apartments and a disabled-accessible room. A buffet breakfast, included in the room rate, is served in one of the hotel's two restaurants. The larger of the two, located in the hotel's cellar,

HOTELS

seats 150 people and is available for parties and banquets.

Hotel Salvator
$$$ **35 rooms**
Truhlářská 10. 222 312 234.
www.salvator.cz.
The majority of rooms in this Listed Historic Building face the inner landscaped courtyard, where guests can enjoy breakfast, weather permitting. The adjoining restaurant, La Boca, boasts a garden terrace and a billiards room. Accommodations here are spacious, bright and clean, with a level of quality commensurate with the price – which ends up feeling like a great deal. A bonus for families: children under age 11 stay for free.

Hotel Yasmin
$$$ **196 rooms**
Politických vězňů 12. 234 100 100.
www.hotel-yasmin.cz.
Located only steps away from historic Wenceslas Square, this hotel provides spacious and clean rooms at a reasonable rate. All rooms have free Wi-Fi, and two rooms are customized for disabled guests. **Yasmin Noodles ($$)** serves noodle dishes from all over the world as well as a buffet-style breakfast each morning. The hotel also includes a small fitness center.

Mosaic House
$$$ **94 rooms**
Odboru 4. 246 008 324.
www.mosaichouse.com.
This fully air-conditioned hotel and hostel prides itself on its green credentials and was selected as a finalist for the Eco Energy Award for 2011. **Belushi's Bar and Restaurant ($$)**, attached to the hotel, offers killer burgers and a fun place to watch the latest sports match.

Sheraton Hotel
$$$ **160 rooms**
Žitná 8. 225 999 999.
www.sheratonprague.com.
Boasting all the amenities that you would expect from the Sheraton, the Prague version also claims very reasonable rates. In addition to the bar and restaurant on the ground floor, there are meeting rooms and a small fitness center (free for guests) . A buffet breakfast is included in the price of select rooms.

Mosaic House

©Cat Norman/Mosaic House

Hotel Imperial
$$$$$ **126 rooms**
Na Poříčí 5. 246 011 440.
www.hotel-imperial.cz.
Wrap yourself in Art Deco splendor at this 1914 property, one of the most prestigious establishments in the city. Custom-made furnishings, original artwork and high ceilings deck the rooms out in style, while services encompass a spa and a fitness center with personal trainers at your beck and call. Traditional Czech cuisine is updated with a contemporary flair at the hotel's elegant **Café Imperial ($$$)**.

Le Palais
$$$$$ **73 rooms**
U Zvonařky 1. 234 634 111.
www.palaishotel.cz.
One of Prague's most luxurious boutique hotels, Le Palais sees to guests' comfort in individually decorated rooms and suites, all with high-speed Internet access, DVD players and marble bathrooms with heated floors. Kick up the luxe factor in a room with a balcony or fireplace and a frescoed ceiling. When you're not in your room, work out in the health center or relax at Pure Spa. **Le Papillon ($$$)** serves innovative Bohemian dishes.

Greater Prague

Czech Inn Hostel
$ **35 rooms**
Francouzská 76, Vinohrady.
267 267 612. www.czech-inn.com.
If you're traveling on a strict budget, this hostel with its friendly staff is for you. Inexpensive rooms range from shared dorms (269 Kč) to private apartments (1,567 Kč). In the evening, you may end up just lounging in the bar/café and listening to some of the live music that plays there on a regular basis. Even though the buffet breakfast is not included in the price of the room, the Czech is nonetheless a good deal.

Hotel Amadeus
$ **50 rooms**
Dalimilova 10, Žižkov. 222 780 267.
www.amadeushotel.cz.
Amadeus offers a bargain in the über-trendy Žižkov neighborhood, with loads of nightclubs, pubs and cafés only a few minutes' walk away. Accommodations are divided between standard rooms and apartments (breakfast included in the rate for both), housed in two adjoining buildings. Studio and two-bedroom apartments all come equipped with kitchenettes.

Hotel Amadeus

©Vesta Travel Agency/Hotel Amadeus

Sir Toby's Hostel
$ **8 rooms**
Delnická 24, Holešovice. 246 032 610. www.sirtobys.com.
For a lively, friendly budget experience, Sir Toby's is the place. Shared dorms (including single-sex options) with shared bathrooms as well as private rooms for up to three people offer hardwood floors and tasteful décor. Some have private ensuite bathrooms. Sir Toby's offers free

HOTELS

Wi-Fi throughout the hostel, as well as complimentary tea and a continental breakfast for a small fee. When you just want to hang out, there's a pleasant garden area outside and a lively pub downstairs, which often features live music.

Aparthotel Gregory
$$ 7 rooms
Ameriká 16, Vinohrady. 269 335 060. www.pension-apartment.cz.
Ideal for families or longer stays, this Aparthotel calls the leafy, residential district of Vinohrady home. The property, which offers both double rooms and spacious apartments (some accommodating up to 10 guests) with kitchenettes, is convenient to the neighborhood's pubs, restaurants and bars. Breakfast is not included in the cost of a room, but the hotel offers outstanding comfort for this price range.

Aparthotel Na Bělidle
$$ 30 rooms
Na Bělidle 27, Smíchov. 222 522 508. www.pension-apartment.cz.
Though not exactly in the center of the city, the Na Bělidle is only a few steps from the river, and close to the Nový Smíchov shopping center. And it's close to trams and metro stations for touring the city.
With room options ranging from a studio to a family-sized apartment, this is a great place to stay when you're on a budget. Attractive rooms come with complimentary Internet access. Breakfast is available for a fee of 70 Kč per person per day.

Apartments Vyšehrad
$$ 10 apartments
Vratislavova 17/38, Albertov. 224 915 150. www.apart-vysehrad.cz.
These tastefully decorated apartments sit at the foot of the remains of the early-18C Vyšehrad Fortress, just outside the city center. Staying here gives guests a chance to discover the neighborhood of Albertov, an authentic and vibrant residential quarter. A great value for the price, rooms here come with or without kitchenettes, and all have writing desks. The hotel provides a buffet breakfast for an extra 150 Kč.

©Apartments Vyšehrad

Hotel Dalimil
$$ 53 rooms
Prokopovo nám 2-3, Žižkov. 222 539 539. www.dalimilhotel prague.com.
Only 10 minutes from the center of Prague by tram, this hip neighborhood offers loads of local color, and the adjoining streets teem with typical pubs to stop in for a beer. Small but well-appointed rooms have retro furnishings with simple lines. A vaulted dining room and tables set up in the courtyard in the summer are both pleasant places to enjoy the complimentary morning buffet.

Hotel Diplomat

$$ 398 rooms

Evropska 15, Dejvice. 296 539 111.
www.diplomathotel.cz.

The Diplomat shines for its competitive rates and top-quality services, all within easy reach of both the airport and Prague city center. All rooms feature air-conditioning, minibars, satellite flat-screen TVs, DVD players and high-speed Internet access; some of the suites have views of nearby Prague Castle. There are three restaurants onsite, as well as a café, and the expansive conference facilities can cater events for up to 1,050 people. Coffee and tea come compliments of the house, but breakfast is not included.

Arcadia Residence

$$$ 12 apartments

Hostivítova 3, Vyšehrad. 724 027 525. www.arcadiaresidence.com.

Offering studio apartments, one- and two-bedroom apartments as well as attic rooms, Arcadia Residence is equally suitable for singles as well as large families. Although it is an apartment hotel (all rooms are equipped with kitchenettes), the Arcadia offers many amenities that you would expect from a full-service property, such as breakfast, laundry facilities, maid service, tourist information and more.

Golden Well Hotel

$$$$$ 19 rooms

U Zlaté studně 4, Hradčany.
257 011 213. www.goldenwell.cz.

A hidden gem, this 16C Renaissance building lies below the walls of Prague Castle, close to the best sights of the Lesser Town, such as Charles Bridge and Kampa Park. Connecting grand deluxe rooms on the third floor can easily accommodate families; some of the smaller rooms face the cobblestone courtyard. Thoughtful extras include turn-down service, a pillow menu and morning newspaper delivered to your room, while bathrooms have luxuries like Jacuzzi tubs and heated floors. Ask the staff to arrange private guided tours of the city, and check out the rooftop terrace for magnificent views over the city.

Hotel General

$$$$$ 20 rooms

Svornosti 10, Smíchov. 257 318 320.
www.hotel-general.com.

As its name implies, the General fashions its rooms and public spaces with famous military leaders in mind. You'll be offered a welcome drink before checking into your elegantly appointed, air-conditioned room. The hotel sauna is available to guests any time of the day for an hourly fee, and the buffet breakfast is on the house. If you want to see the sights, this luxury boutique property is close to major Metro and tram stops, so getting around the city is a breeze. Check the hotel's website for advanced booking specials offering discounts of up to 50 percent.

Hotel General

©Hotel General

PRAGUE

 **NOTES**